Counterstorytelling Narratives
of Latino Teenage Boys

Critical
Studies of
LATINOS/AS
in the
Americas

Yolanda Medina and Margarita Machado-Casas
General Editors

Vol. 8

The Critical Studies of Latinos/as in the Americas series
is part of the Peter Lang Trade Academic and Textbook list.
Every volume is peer reviewed and meets
the highest quality standards for content and production.

PETER LANG
New York • Bern • Frankfurt • Berlin
Brussels • Vienna • Oxford • Warsaw

Juan A. Ríos Vega

Counterstorytelling Narratives of Latino Teenage Boys

From *Vergüenza* to *Échale Ganas*

PETER LANG
New York • Bern • Frankfurt • Berlin
Brussels • Vienna • Oxford • Warsaw

Library of Congress Cataloging-in-Publication Data
Ríos Vega, Juan A.
Counterstorytelling narratives of Latino teenage boys:
from vergüenza to échale ganas / Juan A. Ríos Vega.
pages cm. — (Critical studies of Latino/as in the Americas; vol. 8)
Includes bibliographical references.
1. Hispanic American teenage boys—Education (Secondary)—United States.
2. Latin Americans—Education (Secondary)—United States. 3. Teenage immigrants—
Education (Secondary)—United States. 4. Latin Americans—Ethnic identity.
5. Discrimination in education—United States. 6. Racism—United States. I. Title.
LC2670.4.R56   371.829'68073—dc23   2015019987
ISBN 978-1-4331-3039-7 (hardcover)
ISBN 978-1-4331-3038-0 (paperback)
ISBN 978-1-4539-1671-1 (e-book)
ISSN 2372-6822 (print)
ISSN 2372-6830 (online)

Bibliographic information published by **Die Deutsche Nationalbibliothek**.
Die Deutsche Nationalbibliothek lists this publication in the "Deutsche
Nationalbibliografie"; detailed bibliographic data are available
on the Internet at http://dnb.d-nb.de/.

The paper in this book meets the guidelines for permanence and durability
of the Committee on Production Guidelines for Book Longevity
of the Council of Library Resources.

© 2015 Peter Lang Publishing, Inc., New York
29 Broadway, 18th floor, New York, NY 10006
www.peterlang.com

Printed in the United States of America

CONTENTS

PREFACE

My ESL classroom was always in the basement or in a trailer. It was always invisible to many other students and teachers. Even some of my students who did not want to be labeled as different or dumb for not speaking English sometimes recognized the stigma of an ESL classroom.

It was in my second year of teaching at a middle school when I met Santiago and Ana (pseudonyms). Both siblings came from a rural area in Mexico. Santiago was born in Texas but his parents took him and the rest of the family back to Mexico when they were infants. Santiago was the oldest of his three brothers and the third of six children. Santiago, who looked like a country Mexican boy, was amazed to be in a new school and meeting new friends, especially girls. Since he was a very good-looking boy, it was not that difficult for other Mexican girls to be attracted to him. However, his lack of the English language got him in trouble many times. Santiago was always bullied for wearing a black leather jacket or "guaraches" (Mexican sandals) or for speaking Spanish with an "acento ranchero" (country accent), but he never let others make fun of him. Instead, he always fought back on the bus and the cafeteria, both before and after school. Santiago was always in the office, and punished with In-School Suspension (ISS) and Out-of-School Suspension (OSS). I talked to him many times, but it was difficult for him to understand how to play the education system (conformity = invisibility) in this country. Shortly afterward, Santiago was constantly targeted at school, causing him to become an outcast.

One day the SRO, a Black woman, came to my small ESL classroom to let me know that Santiago was in serious trouble. She shared with me Santiago's incident. This time Santiago was accused of harassing a white girl. What Santiago did not realize this time was that the girl he had harassed was the high school principal's daughter. Santiago was in serious trouble. The SRO told me that Santiago only had two options; attend a juvenile boot camp, or be expelled from school. For these reasons, she wanted me to contact Santiago's parents since they did not speak English. She also shared with me a list of things Santiago's parents would need to buy if they agreed to send Santiago to the boot camp.

That afternoon I visited Santiago's parents and explained his situation to them. I let them know that it was very important to keep Santiago in school since he was still a minor. Santiago's parents were scared about the whole situation and decided to send him to boot camp. However, they did not have the monetary resources to purchase the required supplies (white clothes, sheets, and underwear). I took the list and headed to Wal-Mart. The next day, I showed up at Santiago's house and dropped off some bags. When Santiago's parents asked me where I had gotten the money to buy all of the supplies, I said, "I stood by the door at Wal-Mart and asked for donations." I guessed they figured out that I was not telling the truth.

With limited English, Santiago was sent to boot camp for over a month. He had to get up early in the morning to exercise and to help in the kitchen. He also had to take classes and to do community service. Santiago did an outstanding job at the camp. I was told that other boys cried so much that their parents had to take them home, while some others were injured, but Santiago was determined to do his best.

Before the end of boot camp, Santiago's parents called and invited me to Santiago's graduation ceremony. It was a very hot afternoon in June. I took my camera and a present. I have to confess that I felt like crying many times when I saw Santiago dressed in white with the rest of the boys. Amazingly, Santiago's behavior and leadership skills were acknowledged that afternoon. Santiago was chosen to lead his team in a karate routine. Like his parents, I felt so proud of him. After my third year, I had to say goodbye to Santiago and Ana since my contract as an exchange teacher was at an end. I left that school system with good and bad memories about the experiences of students like Santiago who had a hard time adapting to the dominant culture.

When I finally had a chance to change my immigration status, I got a job at a different school system within the same county. To my surprise, one of my Latina students was Santiago's girlfriend. Through her, I learned that Santiago had finished high school and decided to become a police officer. I also learned that Santiago and my student had a permanent relationship.

Thanks to Facebook, I have been able to reconnect with Santiago and his wife. They have two cute children and are still together. Santiago resigned his job as a police officer since it kept him away from home. He is working at a local construction company and taking care of his wife and children. I will always remember Santiago as a strong student. Even though he challenged social expectations, his determination and support from others allowed him to overcome life's obstacles.

As a teacher and community leader, I witnessed many stories with tragic outcomes. I saw many Latino teenage boys expelled from school for gang affil-iations, drugs, or getting into trouble for breaking the law. Some others con-sidered education a waste of time. Instead, they decided to join their parents, relatives, and other dropout friends in supporting their parents and younger siblings. However, I also experienced seeing Latino boys—who had to nego-tiate and sometimes risk their cultural identities in order to go against the norm—succeed academically.

The genesis of this book started in my ESL classroom where my students and I found a nest to nurture one another. This space allowed us to share our frustrations, commonalities, and happiness as immigrants, second-language learners, and brownness in this country. My students and I developed a sense of *familia* (family). I heard their stories of sacrifice and loyalty to their loved ones. I came to understand how and why their parents left everything behind to come to this country. I learned to find *esperanza* (hope) even in the most difficult days. It was through the use of dialogue journals (which I still keep as priceless treasures), community service projects, school, and community cultural events that I decided to document the stories of my students. It was my frustrations and pains as an immigrant man that pushed me to echo my students' narratives.

After teaching at the same high school for over ten years, sometimes feel-ing more oppressed than my students, I decided to quit my teaching job and become a full-time doctoral student. After long conversations with friends, colleagues, and my advisor, I resigned from my teaching job. It was a very traumatic decision—emotionally and financially—but I wanted to focus on my doctoral studies and to gain experience teaching undergraduate students.

I also left my classroom and my students behind to accomplish my mission of echoing their experiences of hard work, invisibility, and resiliency.

During my last year of teaching, I shared with my students my idea about writing a book about them. When I asked some of them if they were willing to help me, they all agreed to participate. As a result, some of their stories are shared here. My Latino/a students and their families have become the inspiring impetus to write this book. They have made me not only a better teacher and scholar, but *un mejor ser humano* (a better human being).

I hope this book will allow many readers to better understand the educational experiences of many Latinos/as in this country.

Señor Ríos, que alegría tan grande de saber que esta a punto de empezar un capítulo nuevo en su vida, me da mucho gusto saber que de alguna manera dejamos una huella en su vida, grandiosa la vida que puso a tan gran persona y maestro en nuestros caminos, quizas nunca lo demostramos, quizas en tiempos pasado no entendíamos todo lo que nos quería enseñar con su consejos, pero usted siempre tuvo gran influencia en nuestras vidas, y de alguna manera aún lo sigue haciendo ... me siento afortunado de haberlo tenido como maestro y muy orgulloso de que aún lo sigamos teniendo de inspiración para seguir adelante en los sueños que tenemos ... Le deseo lo mejor.

Mr. Ríos, I am so happy to know that you are about to start a new chapter in your life. I am so happy to know that we left footprints in your life, life has been grateful by bringing a wonderful person and teacher to our life journeys, maybe we never showed it to show, maybe during those times we did not understand what you wanted to teach us through your advice, but you still had a lot of influence in our lives, and you still do in a certain way. I feel very fortunate for having you as a teacher, I am very proud that we are still inspired by you while moving ahead with our dreams ... I wish you the best.

—Lino Julian Sanchez,
a former student, is currently studying medicine in Mexico.

ACKNOWLEDGMENTS

An individual's accomplishment is not based on a single effort but on a supportive system of people that allows it to become true. I am so thankful for having people who supported me in writing this book. For that reason, I want to thank my mother, Deisy, for being my first teacher, role model, and hero; my siblings Diana and Emiliano for showing society that we are the only crafters of our own life outcomes; and my nephews Luis, Damian, and Darness for giving me the strength to complete this project.

I am deeply honored to thank Yajaira Ascencio Owens for helping me to recruit the participants in this book. I want to thank Rausie Hubson, my colleague and friend, for her willingness to proofread my first rough drafts and for giving me down-to-earth input. I want to thank Dr. Jean Aguilar-Valdez for reading my first chapters and introducing me to new scholars and studies that helped shape my book writing.

I thank Dr. Silvia Bettez, my professor, advisor, and *amiga* for believing and instilling in me hard work throughout my doctoral studies and book writing; and my professors Dr. Svi Shapiro, Dr. Ye He, and Dr. Leila Villaverde for their words of encouragement before and during my book writing. Thanks for pushing me to analyze society with a critical lens.

I also want to thank Dr. David Stovall, my mentor, and Yolanda Medina, my book editor, for their words of wisdom and friendship during my book editing. I want to thank the Nolan family: Bob, Shirley, Hollis, and Rob, for being my biggest supporters during and after my book writing.

Finally, I want to thank all of my Latino/a students and their families, whose stories and cultural wealth became the inspiration for this book. Thanks for letting me feel *como en casa* (like home).

FROM *VERGÜENZA* TO *ÉCHALE GANAS*

Cuando mis padres me despertaron esa noche sentí que la aventura mas maravillosa estaba a punto de comenzar. Esos días en el desierto, cruzando desoladas tierras y un caudaloso río parecían las cosas mas difíciles para alcanzar el sueño Americano de mis padres, a écharle ganas para un mejor mañana.

(*When my parents woke me up late at night, I felt the most wonderful adventure was about to start. Days in the desert or crossing a desolated desert and a dangerous river will be my most difficult things to achieve my parents' American dream of doing the best for a better future.*)

Mi nueva vida, mejor educación, una casa decente, y ropas de marca soñaban como palabras mágicas para mis oídos. El niño pobre de rancho quien solía soñar con Los Guardianes de la Bahía y super heroes de la televisión finalmente estaría en El Norte. Sin embargo, mi aventura giró al revés una vez que mi familia y yo cruzamos la frontera.

(*New life, better education, a decent house, and fancy clothes sounded like magical words to my ears. The poor niño de rancho who used to dream about Bay Watch and super heroes from TV will finally be en El Norte. However, my adventure turned upside-down once my family and I crossed la frontera.*)

Are you Latino, Hispanic, or Mexican? Are you illegal? When are you going back home? Do your parents pay taxes? How many people live in that house? When are you and your people gonna stop coming? Are you and your people planning to stay here forever?

For others I am Mexican, even though my family came from Nicaragua, El Salvador, Honduras, Costa Rica, Guatemala, or Panama; all of them for different reasons, but still for them I am Mexican, the one who is not gonna graduate from high school, the trouble maker, the outcast, the dark skin, the wetback, the gang member, and drunk.

Even though I have tried to fit into this new and oppressive world, I am consciously aware that for me to do it I will end up losing many things that make me proud of where I came from; my romantic language, the respect adults deserve, my family values, the family recipe to make real tamales, the love for my *cumbia, los corridos, los cuentos de la abuela, las ferias, las quermeses, y el amor a su tierra*.

Now, I speak the language of the oppressor, but I cannot deny who I am; just another immigrant, trying to survive in a foreign land and away from home. Maybe someday when I am old and tired, I will be back to the land I was unearthed from when I was still innocent, but now this sense of fear is back again.

What will I decide to do with my life, *solo Dios sabe*. I will try to be patient enough to learn how to navigate the world of the oppressor, but never, never forget who I am, just another, Latino, Hispanic, or Mexican immigrant in this fanaticized world where many would like to come, make *mucho dinero y regresar a su tierra antes que nos alcance la muerte*.

· 1 ·

LATINO BOYS'
COUNTERSTORYTELLING

Students of color are allowed to enter the classroom but never on an equal footing. When they walk in, they are subject to the same racial stereotypes and expectations that exist in the larger society. Students of color do not have the advantage of walking into a classroom as individuals; they walk in as black, brown, or red persons with all the connotations such racialization raises in the classroom. They do not walk into a classroom where the curriculum embraces their histories. They walk into a classroom where their histories and cultures are distorted, where they feel confused about their own identities, vulnerabilities, and oppressions. (Zamudio, Russell, Rios, & Bridgeman, 2011, pp. 18–19)

This book echoes the voices of many U.S.-born Latino[1] and Latino immigrant teenage boys in this country whose idea of getting an education for the betterment of their *familias* becomes a myth once their ethnic/cultural identities and gender are shaped by socio-historical constructs used in a culture of whiteness to oppress and to marginalize Communities of Color. Drawing on critical race theory (CRT), Latino critical theory (LatCrit), and Chicano/Chicana epistemologies as a theoretical framework, I unpack how nine Latino boys' counterstories, revealing their experiences with race, racism, and gender discrimination, which are usually silenced by majoritarian (quantitative and culturally biased) studies, challenge Latino boys' school failure as a norm. In this book, I want to highlight that the experiences of Latino boys and men in this country are filled with courage, sacrifice, tears, fears, and resilience.

According to the Pew Hispanic Center (2011), never before in this country's history has a minority ethnic group made up so large a share of the youngest Americans. The 2010 Census counted 50.5 million Latinos, making up 16.3% of the total population. From 35.3 million in 2000, Latinos grew 43% by 2010. Among children ages 17 and younger, there were 17.1 million Latinos in 2010 or 23% of this age group. Unfortunately, the U.S. Census Bureau (2008) showed that Latinos were more likely to be in the dropout pool than other students, 17% compared to 5% of non-Latino white students, 4% of Asian students, and 9% of Black students. It is clear that many of today's Latino youth, especially teenage boys, are struggling to navigate two worlds. Noguera and Hurtado (2012) state that there has been no social movement initiated to address the disproportionate academic failure of Latino boys or men; they argue that one of the reasons is because white men have not felt the need to address the issue since they still form the majority of men in the United States. For that reason, it is extremely important to hear and analyze how Latino youth's personal experiences in education affect their academic achievement and personal lives.

Theoretical Frameworks

The primary operating frames for the remainder of the book draw from critical race theory (CRT), Latino critical theory (LatCrit), and Chicano/Chicana epistemologies. Through a CRT lens, I explore how racism shapes these boys' experiences in education. Using CRT and LatCrit that recognize communities of color as "holders and creators of knowledge" (Delgado Bernal, 2002), the book centralizes the participants' stories and life experiences as boys and men of color living in the United States.

Using LatCrit to challenge issues of language, immigration, ethnicity, culture, multi-identity, phenotype, and sexuality in Latino/Latina immigrants, issues that have been ignored by most critical race scholars (Solórzano & Delgado Bernal, 2001), the book examines how race and racism shape these Latino boys' experiences in school. Drawing from Chicano/Chicana epistemologies (Delgado Bernal, 1998, Solórzano & Delgado Bernal, 2001), I seek to challenge issues of oppression related to race, class, gender, sexuality, nation of origin, age, and ethnicity. I also unveil how the participants use certain cultural capital as a springboard to develop resiliency while developing a network of support allowing them to stay in school (Stanton-Salazar, 1997; Stanton-Salazar & Spina, 2000). In addition, Chicano/Chicana epistemologies also address experiences with racism as they intersect other forms of oppression such as immigration status, migration, skin color, generational status, bilingualism, limited English proficiency, and the contradictions of Catholicism. A Chicano/Chicana epistemology lens allows me to examine how these young men and their parents' immigration and socioeconomic status as well as language acquisition intersect with issues of racism and discrimination, which push them to be part of a minority caste throughout the U.S.

CRT/LatCrit and Chicano/Chicana epistemologies are useful in the exploration of institutional practices and policies that interfere with the educational experiences of Latino teenage boys. These theoretical perspectives help me to explore the relationship between the historical and contemporary nature of racism and the social construction of race, gender, and other forms of oppression. They also allow me to unveil how notions of gender and practices of racism are instrumental in understanding oppression and racial inequality among Latino teenage boys and men of color.

Motivations for the Remainder of This Book

Using CRT and LatCrit in education, and Chicano/Chicana, Latino teenage boys' counter-narratives, the remainder of the manuscript attempts to address the following questions:

1. How do educational structures, practices, and discourses perpetuate elements of meritocracy, color-blindness, race neutrality, and inequality among Latino teenage boys?
2. How do the interrelations of racism, gender discrimination, and other forms of subordination shape the educational experiences of Latino teenage boys?
3. How can the community cultural wealth of Latino teenage boys be used as a catalyst to secure their academic success?

These research questions allowed me to craft comprehensive individual interview and focus groups questions.

Interrogating My Positionality

Claiming myself as a postcritical ethnographer, I was conscious of my positionality and reflexivity as I shared part of my own biography with the young men I interviewed. Noblit, Flores, and Murillo (2004) agree that postcritical ethnographers have to acknowledge that our own biographies, cultures, and historical contexts matter since they "determine what we see and don't see, understand and not understand, our ability to analyze and not analyze, to disseminate knowledge adequately or not" (p. 34).

As a Latino male from a working-class background, to some I represent an "insider." I also have a connection to some of the students as their former teacher. Being born in a male-dominant Latin American country, during my childhood I was marginalized for being raised by a single and overprotective mother.

Simultaneously, I am also aware of my role as an "outsider" (former teacher, community leader, professional, middle-class, middle-aged, researcher) in relation to the students. In addition, I am critically conscious of being an "outsider" to the dominant culture since I have also experienced oppression for being a Latino male immigrant, having what some consider a "strong accent" when speaking English. I have been racially profiled as an undocumented immigrant and/or drug dealer on more than one occasion by police patrols, immigration and customs agents, and racist locals. In all of these instances I have to remind myself that my personal emotions help me identify when my subjectivities are engaged. It is my subjectivity as an "insider" and "outsider" to both the participants and the dominant culture that helped me explore my own feelings in relationship to what I learned about myself and what kept me from learning. Glesne (2006) argues that the goal of subjectivity is to explore what your feelings tell you about who you are in relationship to what you are learning and to what you may be keeping yourself from learning. Since the subject of the book is closely related to my personal and professional life, I realize that I have to pay constant attention to my subjectivity.

Using Delgado Bernal's (1998) *cultural intuition* as part of my researcher positionality, I analyzed the students' counterstories. *Cultural intuition* "extends one's personal experience to include collective experience and community memory, and points to the importance of participants' engaging in the analysis of data" (pp. 563–564). Giroux (2012a) posits "when our experiences are connected to history, they carry an insightful narrative, allowing us to link the personal to the political while they also push us to translate private issues into public considerations" (p. 28). I bring *cultural intuition* as a Latino male with counterstories of my own, as well as over 15 years of experience working with and for students of color and adults in secondary and postsecondary institutions.

I am also aware of my role as *la callejera*/the streetwalker (Lugones, 2003). For Lugones (2003), the streetwalker/*la callejera* possesses a "multiplicity and depth of perception and connection and hangs out even in well-defined institutional spaces, troubling and subverting their logics" (p. 224). It is the streetwalker who "develops an ear and a tongue for the multiple lines of meaning" (p. 224). The streetwalker creates a "vivid sense of the inadequacy of an individualistic understanding of agency, intentionality, and meaning to one's situation" (p. 225). The streetwalker theorist uncovers, considers, and passes on knowledge of the different tools of tactical strategists by having an in-depth understanding of social structure. It was my role as *la callejera* that also led me to share with the students some of my stories of oppression and resistance as a Latino immigrant man, teacher, and scholar.

Additionally, I was conscious that my position of privilege as an interviewer impacted my behavior and language during the interviews and observations. Glesne (2006) suggests that researchers use their feelings to inquire into our perspectives and interpretations in order to shape new questions through reexamining our assumptions. Monitoring my own subjectivity allowed me to learn more about my own values, attitudes, beliefs, interests, and needs as a researcher. I knew that my subjectivity became the basis for the stories that I am able to tell.

Pillow (2010) defines reflexivity as "an on-going self-awareness during the research process, which aids in making visible the practice and construction of knowledge within research in order to produce more accurate analyses of our research" (p. 274). My reflexivity encouraged me to be self-aware of my political/cultural consciousness and positionality as a Latino male researcher. This awareness led me to keep asking myself questions as I listened to the participants. My reflexivity also led me to ask questions of myself as I wrote my reflections. I tried to determine what in my autobiography shaped my interest in Latino teenage boys; why and where I engaged with them; how my values and experiences shaped my perspectives; and the reason why I chose a particular question in my interviews. My reflexivity as a postcritical ethnographer helped me to assume my responsibility for the world I was producing when I interpreted the participants' counterstories.

Drawing from CRT and LatCrit theories and Chicano/Chicana epistemologies, my goal is to amplify the voices of Latino teenage boys by drawing attention to their experiences in education while challenging previous majoritarian interpretations about this underrepresented group. CRT and LatCrit allows me to examine how the Latino group has been historically marginalized and discriminated against. Finally, using CRT, LaCrit theories and Chicano/Chicana epistemologies, I was able to unpack how these teenagers were able to use their cultural capitals to cope with institutionalized societal barriers while developing resilience and a supporting network orientation.

Students Profiles

I interviewed nine teenagers who all attended the same high school. Fictitious names have been given to protect anonymity in accordance with ethical standards of educational research.

Alex

Alex was born in Long Beach, California, to parents who fled from Guatemala around 20 years ago. His parents split up when he was eight years old. He, his mom, and siblings moved to North Carolina in 1999, where he started his kindergarten education. Alex was 17 years old and a senior. He calls himself Hispanic and has Mesoamerican (indigenous) complexion and has brown skin. I've known Alex since I co-taught his Civics and Economics class two years ago. During that time Alex was a quiet and smart student. However, I knew he had been in trouble at school for gang-related activities. His father lived in Texas and came to visit twice a year. Alex worked at a fast-food restaurant after school and on weekends.

Carlos

Carlos's parents came from the Dominican Republic at a young age. Carlos is a brown-skinned boy. His mother came when she was 12 years old and completed high school in the United States; his father came during his adolescence and did not attend high school since he had to work from his early childhood back in his country. Carlos was born in Manhattan, New York, and raised in New Jersey. His parents divorced when he was six years old. Then two years ago Carlos, his mom, and his younger sister migrated south. He transferred to this school at the end of his sophomore year. At the time of our conversations Carlos was 17 years old and a senior. He used various terms to describe his background including Dominican, Hispanic, and Latin. He was more fluent in English than in Spanish. His father still lived and worked in New Jersey. Carlos and his father maintained a very close relationship.

Emilio

I met Emilio through one of his teachers and counselor. Emilio's parents came from Cuba when they were 18 years old. Emilio was born in Florida and then moved to North Carolina with his parents when he was three years old. At the time of our conversations, Emilio was 15 years old and a freshman. During my interviews, I realized that I had taught some of his relatives. Emilio, who called himself both Latino and Hispanic, was a brown-skinned boy.

José

José's father migrated to the United States years before he decided to bring the rest of his family. José, a brown-skinned boy, was born in Mexico City and moved to the U.S. when he was eight years old. At that time, José started attending fourth grade. José has always liked to dress well and to play soccer. He was 14 years old and a sophomore, and used to be one of my ESL students. I met José's mother at a community event held to assist Latino youth fill out the Deferred Action forms that would allow undocumented youth to have access to a driver's license and to get a job. José still struggles with the English language; therefore, he still receives ESL services.

Juan

I have known Juan's parents and siblings for many years, but he was never my student. Juan was 15 years old and a sophomore. He was born in Veracruz, Mexico, and immigrated to the United States when he was three years old. Juan had a Mesoamerican (indigenous) complexion and a darker shade of brown than the rest of the boys. He is the youngest of four children: three boys and one girl. All of his siblings were labeled English Language Learners (ELLs) and Exceptional Children (EC), so their schooling experiences were not academically successful. His older brother, who was labeled ESL and EC, got into numerous fights and had drug-related problems. He was punished in school and sent to jail many times until he was finally deported back to Mexico. Of all the participants, Juan experienced more oppression than the rest due to issues of phenotype, class, and immigration status. However, he was still trying to overcome those obstacles. During our conversations, I learned that Juan did not live with his biological parents due to some problems with his oldest brother, which I will address later in the book.

Julio

Julio, a light-skinned teenage boy, was born in Colombia and came to the U.S. when he was two years old. Before moving to the South, he and his family lived in New York. Both of his parents finished high school in Colombia. Initially his parents immigrated to the United States for a couple of months; then they went back to pick up Julio and his older sister. I met Julio through his sister, who used to take the ESL state tests during the spring every year until she graduated. Julio is a white-complexioned teenager who easily blends in with the rest of the white students. He called himself Latino, Hispanic, and Colombian.

Luis

I met Luis during my last year of teaching when I co-taught his English II course. I always admired him for being in school after he became a young father at the age of 15. At the time of our conversations, Luis was 17 years old and a senior. He was born and raised in the South, where he attended school. He was a brown-skinned boy. His parents came from two different states in Mexico, Guerrero and Estado de Mexico. Before migrating to the South, Luis's mother lived in California and his father lived in Chicago. They moved to North Carolina because they had family members living here. He had been punished at school many times for being resistant to teachers and school administrators' norms. Previous to our conversations, I was told that Luis was suspended for 10 days due to some bullying problems on a school bus. Luis worked after school and on weekends at a pizza restaurant. He also enjoyed playing soccer at school and was in a community league.

Pedro

I met Pedro when I co-taught his English 10 course. Pedro was 17 years old and a junior. His parents came from El Salvador. He was born in California and moved to the South when he was five years old. Pedro called himself American. He had a light skin tone. He was more fluent in English than in

Spanish; he could understand Spanish but his Spanish speaking and writing skills were minimal. Pedro had always been a very respectful and athletic teenager, but his academic performance made him an average student. During our conversations I learned that Pedro's parents separated and that his father's absence deeply affects him. Pedro is the only boy in the family; he has two sisters and he's the middle child. His older sister, who was 18 years old at the time and a senior, was expecting a baby. Pedro is very close to his mother. As the only male, he has to perform the masculine role and support his mother and younger sister around the house.

Raúl

Raúl was 17 years old and a senior. He self-identified as Puerto Rican and also American. He attended my ESL class last year. Since he recently moved from Puerto Rico, his English skills were still very limited. Raúl attended ninth and 10th grades back in Puerto Rico; he was placed in 11th grade even though he was a novice English language learner. Most of our interviews were held in Spanish or code-switched in both languages (Spanish-English). Raúl was very quiet and smart. When he first came to the school his peers, teachers, and school administrators assumed that he was African American because of his physical appearance and mixed (Black-brown) skin tone. In addition, when speaking in Spanish some of his Latino peers used to make fun of him because of the Caribbean rhythm of his speech.

Additionally, I decided to interview eight teachers and to find out about their experiences teaching Latino boys in high school. The table below shows a more detailed description of the teachers.

Table 1. Teachers' Profiles.

Teacher	Race/Ethnicity	Subject	Years of Teaching
Ms. Cook	White	Biology/Chemistry	10
Ms. Dixon	White	English	5
Mr. Hunt	Black	JROTC	19
Mr. Moose	White	Business	9
Mr. Otto	White	U.S. History	13
Mr. Rivers	White	Algebra	13
Mr. Sanchez	Light-Skinned Latino	ESL	7
Ms. Wolf	White	English	10

Interpreting Latinos/as Education Failure

Racism is about institutional power, and people of color in the United States have never possessed this form of power. (Solórzano & Yosso, 2009 p. 24)

Drawing from ethnic studies, the book is situated within the lenses of critical race theory (CRT), Latino critical theory (LatCrit), and Chicano/Chicana epistemologies. Historically, majoritarian studies use a deficient theory model in education to interpret school failure among Communities of Color.

A Deficit-Thinking Model in Education

Drawing on Valencia's (2010) work, scholars, educators, and policymakers have interpreted school failure among low-SES students of color from a deficit-thinking model, which "posits that the student who fails in school does it because of his/her internal deficits or deficiencies." He argues, "from the early 1600s to the late 1800s, a deficit thinking model has become an endogenous theory" (p. 6); perpetuating the idea that minorities are born deficient. Valencia (2010) claims six characteristics of deficit thinking in schooling:

(1) victim blaming: students are blamed based on group membership,
(2) oppression: there is little hope and possibility of success for these students,
(3) pseudoscience: researchers' embedded negative biases toward communities of color,
(4) temporal changes: depends on history, low-grade genes, inferior culture and class, and family organization,
(5) educability: perceptions of low-SES students of color, and
(6) heterodoxy: reflects the dominant, conventional scholarly and ideological climates of the time. (p. 18)

This model of analyzing minorities of color as culturally deficient has led school systems to create school initiatives to support some poor and minority students as "No Child Left Behind," "at risk," "Race to the Top," and "closing the achievement gap." In North Carolina, for example, some racially segregated and low-performance schools are referred as "mission possible schools." In order to attract teachers and school administrators to teach in these underperforming and segregated schools, the Department of Public Instruction allocates monetary supplements for increasing students' testing scores. This idea of increasing low-performing students' scores in a white-dominant school system re-emphasizes the idea of poor students and students of color as culturally deficient.

Valencia and Solórzano (1997) claim that through history majoritarian scholars (Dunn, 1987; Heller, 1996; Jensen, 1969; Terman, 1916) have associated school failure among students of color as biological and genetic. They argue that these studies have analyzed Mexicans', Blacks', and Native Americans' failure in school and found them to be biologically deficient in relation to whites. Valencia and Solórzano (1997) state, "what some scholars originally attributed to biology and genetics of students of color were reclassified and described as cultural deficits" (p. 30). Labeling minorities of color as culturally deficient is still used in our educational systems through multiple remediation, after-school, and summer programs that compare poor minority students with their white peers as the model group.

A deficit-thinking model is also associated with standardized tests and language acquisition. Marx (2006) claims, "deficit thinking is very often perpetuated in colleges of education where pre-service teachers learn that children of color and English-language learners are hard to teach and over-represented in special education and remedial classes" (pp. 53–54). Solórzano and Yosso (2009) claim that current education programs still explore issues of inequity through a model based on the assumption that students of color are culturally deficient. When this idea of a deficit-thinking model is internalized by white Americans as the norm, it is almost impossible to challenge teachers and school administrators to think differently, since they assume that children of color need to be "fixed" or "repaired" in order to succeed academically. Yosso (2006b) suggests that one of the most current forms of racism and discrimination most students of color experience is related to a deficit-thinking model since it blames minority students and their families for their poor academic performance because "(a) students enter school without the normative cultural knowledge and skills, and (b) parents neither value nor support their children's education" (p. 173). In the case of Latino/Latina immigrant students, majoritarian studies (Banfield, 1970; Bernstein, 1977; Schwartz, 1971) argue that the only path for immigrant students to succeed academically is by assimilation into the dominant white culture, "learning English at the expense of losing Spanish and becoming an individual 'American' success story of loosening or cutting family and community ties" (Solórzano & Yosso, 2009, p. 138). When scholars use a deficit thinking model to interpret students' of color school failure and when teachers and school administrators blame Latino/Latina students, their families, cultures, and languages as the reason of school failure, this negative assumption leads most of the students to internalize their cultures as drawbacks against their academic success. Instead, they embrace a white American culture as the only way to succeed academically, sometimes creating an identity crisis.

Critical Race Studies

Several scholars have called for a critical examination of how race and racism are used to subordinate students of color (Bell, 1992; Delgado Bernal, 1998, 2002, 2006; Delgado & Stefancic, 2001; Dixson & Rousseau, 2006; Ladson-Billings & Tate, 2006;, Matsuda, Lawrence, Delgado, & Crenshaw, 1993; Solórzano & Delgado Bernal, 2001; Solórzano & Villalpaldo, 1998; Solórzano & Yosso, 2009; Taylor, Gillborn, & Ladson-Billings, 2009; Valencia, 2010; Yosso, 2006a, 2006b; Zamudio et al., 2011). They agree that the stories of race, racism and other forms of oppression of students of color are often silenced or ignored by blaming the victim as culturally deficient, perpetuating different layers of subordination (racism, classism, sexism, nativism, monolingualism, heterosexism, phenotype, etc.), the myth of meritocracy, and inequality, especially in education. Instead, they suggest that when students of color share their own stories of oppression and discrimination, they can also become creators of their own epistemologies of resistance. These scholars claim that narrating the experiences of students of color with issues of oppression and discrimination in school can allow the participants to figure out their *communal funds of knowledge* (Moll, Amanti, Neff, & Gonzalez, 2009), learn from one another, become *active subjects* (Lugones, 2003) who can develop multiple forms of resistance to succeed academically and socially, and claim for social justice.

Unfortunately, some critical race scholars perpetuate the Black/White binary when analyzing issues of race and racism by lumping Latino/Latina, Blacks, Asian, and Native American students under the umbrella of students of color (Akom, 2008; Bell, 1992; Delpit, 2006, 2012; Ladson-Billings, 2009; Ladson-Billings & Tate, 2006; Ogbu, 2004; Tatum, 1997, 2007; West, 2001, 2004, 2011). Yosso, Smith, Ceja, and Solórzano (2009) argue that "Most public discourse in the United States frames racism as a concern specific to Black and White communities, and higher education tends to replicate this tendency to overlook the racialized histories and experiences of other Communities of Color" (p. 4). I claim that analyzing minorities from Black/White binaries silences the experiences of some Communities of Color that learn to resist and to navigate a white-male dominant society.

Contrary to Black/White binaries in majoritarian ethnic studies, Noguera (2008) challenges Ogbu and Fordham's "acting white" theory stating that some high-achieving minority students become persuaded by the structure and culture of the school, while others learn how to succeed in both worlds by adopting multiple identities (p. 30). Noguera argues that "even if few in number, there are students who manage to maintain their identities and achieve academically without being ostracized by their peers" (p. 32). For that reason, he encourages scholars to analyze how such students learn to navigate the dominant system in order to figure out how to support the academic achievement of more students of color. Following Noguera's argument, my study analyzes how Latino/Chicano families made use of different strategies of resistance while navigating the mainstream culture in the United States.

Current Studies on Mexican, Latino/a, and Chicano/a Families

Common threads emerge in the literature on how Latino/Chicano families use their cultures as assets, challenging quantitative scientific studies that identified Latino/Chicano students and their families as culturally deficient (Suárez-Orozco & Suárez-Orozco, 2001; Suzuki & Valencia, 1997; Valencia, 2010; Valencia & Black, 2002 Valencia & Ronda, 1994). It is important to understand that Latino families do not represent a static and homogenous group. They share some commonalities as immigrants or immigrant descents, Spanish language speakers (some speak indigenous languages), skin color (ranging in appearance as white, black, and *mestizos*), family values and aspirations. However, there is an urgency to analyze their experiences focusing on their differences; their immigration experience before and after they came to this country, as well as issues of race/ethnicity, class, literacy, gender, phenotype, sexual orientation, and religion.

Familism

Valdés's (1996) study on ten Mexican families found that *familism* was very important for the success of immigrant children. She found that the success of the individual did not depend on his/her individualism but on family ties and networks. She posits that the families "had hopes and ambitions ... They fully expected that their children would grow up with the same notions of reciprocity, respect, and responsibility that had been part of their families for generations" (p. 172). Tatum (1997) defines *familism* as a cultural value that provides social support to most Latino families independent of their national background, birthplace, heritage language, or any other socioeconomic characteristic; she claims that "*familism* is not caused by immigration, it is reinforced by it" (p. 137). I claim that *familism* is the best example of a community-oriented society. It is also the way some immigrant families are able to survive and to resist the dominant society, by helping and teaching each other how to navigate the new culture.

It is also important to highlight Valdés's (1996) position on *familism* as a problematic cultural asset based on diverse sociocultural settings. For example, in her study she found that although the ten Mexican families possessed values, beliefs, and social capital that could later turn into economic capitals, they did not figure out how to utilize their *familism* to support their children's education. She argued that even though the Mexican parents in her study valued education they did not understand academic achievement in this country. Her study revealed that there was a disconnect between the school and the Mexican community.

Consejos (Advice or Homilies)

The use of *consejos* (narrative advice or homilies) is commonly used by parents to encourage children to do well in life and school. In Villenas and Deyhle's (1999) *Pedagogies of the Home*, they define *consejos* as "the means by which parents transmit to their children the cultural values and morals that will guide them in good behavior and in making good decisions" (p. 423). They state that many Mexican/Latino parents with low socioeconomic or working-class status and who lack social and cultural capitals to navigate the mainstream society utilize *consejos* as a resource to motivate their children to excel academically. For instance, in some Latin American countries grandparents occupy the highest position in the family since they can give *consejos* based on their lived experiences. Most young generations ask grandparents and parents for *consejos* in order to avoid making mistakes in life. Continuing with Villenas and Deyhle's (1999) dialogue on *consejos*, this study uses Échale ganas (do your best) as a form of *consejo* found in Mexican families to instill in their children the drive to work hard and to do well in school regardless of life's adversities. Échale ganas can also be interpreted as a form of resiliency embedded in the individual's cultural capitals.

Funds of Knowledge

Similar to Villenas and Deyhle's (1999) *Pedagogies of Home* is Moll et al.'s (2009) use of *Funds of Knowledge* as "historically accumulated and culturally developed bodies of knowledge and skills essential for household or individual functioning and well-being" (p. 72). In their study, they analyzed how Mexican families used their funds of knowledge to deal with socio-economic circumstances and built social networks in order to facilitate the development and exchange of resources that allowed them to survive. That development of social networks is connected with the notion of resiliency.

Community Cultural Wealth

Similarly, Tara Yosso's (2006b) Community Cultural Wealth (CCW) explores how the different skills, abilities, and knowledge utilized by Communities of Color allow them to resist different forms of subordination as they navigated a white-male-driven society. Yosso claims that Communities of Color possess cultural wealth grouped in aspirational, navigational, social, linguistic, familial, and resistant forms of capitals. In her study, *Madres por la Educación: Community cultural wealth at Southside Elementary*, Yosso (2006a) analyzed how some Chicana parents use counterstories to unveil their community cultural wealth and to critically analyze their children's marginalization in school for being children of color. Becoming consciously aware of their different cultural capitals led these Chicana mothers to challenge an institutionalized cultural deficit model approach to elementary schooling.

Built on Yosso's Community Cultural Wealth, Pérez Huber's (2009) study of ten Chicana undergraduate students interrogated and challenged the racist nativist framing of undocumented Latino/Latina immigrants. Using CCW, Pérez Huber analyzed how the different forms of capital found within the families and communities of the participants allowed them to survive, resist, and navigate higher education while challenging nativist discourses. Likewise, He, Bettez, and Levin's (2013) unpublished manuscript, using CCW and imagined community-of-education frameworks, explored the educational experiences of immigrants and refugees from China, Mexico, Liberia, and Sudan. Parents described the experiences and fears of their children while attending school in this country. The study showed how children of color were discriminated against based on their ethnicity, language skills, pronunciation, religion, and cultural practices. These different layers of discrimination led parents to internalize a deficit self-perception of their cultural assets. In this study, the researchers challenged the deficit-thinking model in education while offering a model for educators and community members to start more positive changes. At the same time, I found that most of the studies focus on women of color in higher education or as parents. Although my interest was to review previous studies on Latino boys, I found a lack of input that explores the experiences of this group while attending high school in this country. In the next section, I analyze what some have found on issues of gender in Latino/Chicano/Mexican youth.

Gender Studies in Latino/a, Mexican, and Chicano/a Youth in Education

Umaña-Taylor and her colleagues' work (see Alfaro, Umaña-Taylor, Gonzales-Backen, Bámaca, & Zeiders, 2009; Umaña-Taylor, 2004; Umaña-Taylor, Gonzales-Backen, & Guimond, 2009; Umaña-Taylor & Updegraff, 2007) explored identity and self-esteem issues among Latino/Latina youth and how they affected school achievement. They found that Latino/Latina adolescents demonstrate the highest risk for depression among multiple ethnic groups due to discrimination, ethnic processes, and cultural orientations. Other scholars claimed that discrimination is one of the reasons why Latino/Latina youth decide to drop out of school (Pereira, Fuligni, & Potochnick, 2010; Quintana, Segura Herrera, & Nelson, 2010; Zarate, Bhimji, & Reese, 2005); however, focusing mainly on the word "discrimination" could be tricky and problematic since the authors focus only on ethnic/racial discrimination and ignore other types of discrimination related to gender, class, sexual orientation, immigration, phenotype, and language accent.

Other authors have mentioned gender differences between Latino boys and Latina girls in terms of resistance, discrimination, acculturation, academic achievement, gangs, and dropouts (Bettie, 2003; Cammarota, 2008; Flores-González, 2002; López, 2012; Noguera, 2008, 2012; Valencia & Johnson, 2006; Valenzuela, 1999). They have found that immigrant children are not only stereotyped based on their skin color, race, and ethnicity, but also on their gender. Suárez-Orozco, Suárez-Orozco, and Todorova (2008) found that for immigrant children, schools represent "gendered" institutions since Latina girls seem to conform to the system more readily than boys, who are more likely to engage in disruptive behaviors and resistant identities.

"Boys of color, in particular, often face lower expectations, more stigmatiza-
tion, and are subject to more blatant discrimination than girls and are thus at
greater risk for academic disengagement" (Suárez-Orozco et al., 2008, p. 39).
Valenzuela (1999), who studied the academic achievement and schooling
orientations among immigrant Mexican and Mexican American students in
Texas, found that for Mexican American girls, gender represented an addi-
tional form of marginality. Even though they outperformed males academically and saw teachers as caring, their good grades did not mean that Latina
girls did not experience marginality from regular track students. Alfaro et al.
(2009) found that it is important to explore discrimination based on gender
because Latino boys experience more discrimination than Latina girls inside
and outside school settings. They mentioned gender differences relative to
English proficiency and Latino adolescents' academic outcomes. Latino boys
with higher English proficiency reported lower GPAs compared to boys with
lower English proficiency. On the contrary, Latina girls with higher English
proficiency reported higher GPAs when compared to girls with lower English
proficiency. Cammarota (2008), who studied how Latino/Latina youths cope
with economic and political hostilities and work to support their families
while still in school, concludes that the gender differences between Latinos
and Latinas requires further studies that examine the effects of both race and
gender on the development of Latino/Latina youth relationships since for
better or worse Latino/Latina youths' relationships are formed through experiences marked by race and gender.

In Hannah Gill's (2010) book *The Latino Migration Experience in North
Carolina: New Roots in the Old North State*, she analyzes the story of Joe, a
Honduran boy whose parents brought him to the United States when he was
six months old. At the age of 14 Joe decided to drop out of school to help his
single mother pay house bills. She shares that some other Latino/Latina students drop out of school due to lack of access to higher education because of
their legal status, limited English skills, and gangs. She states, "Gangs attract
youth who do not fit in and who seek support and acceptance of peers. Immigrant youth are particularly vulnerable because of xenophobia and exclusion
from mainstream society that they routinely face" (p. 172). Gill (2010) argues
that Latino/Latina youth can become agents of change. Nevertheless, Joe's
experience becomes the norm: "A youth trapped in a lost generation of students unable to attend college" (p. 173). Although she advocates for in-state
tuition for undocumented students, Gill does not explore in-depth how issues
of race, gender, nativism, phenotype, and class intersected in Joe's life.

Also situated in North Carolina, Valencia and Johnson's (2006) quantitative study on Latino/Latina students' experiences of acculturation, school environment, and academic aspirations addressed some gender differences between boys and girls. They found that girls reported more barriers than males within the acculturation process; however, girls showed more academic aspirations, desires to do well in school, and a desire to be successful more than boys; they concluded, "It is clear that being female promotes resiliency with regard to academic aspirations for Latinos/Latinas" (p. 362). Even though this study mentioned discrimination as the most frequently mentioned barrier in school involvement and gender differences between Latino/Latinas in education, it also silenced the students' personal stories by lumping discrimination as a single issue and perpetuating the norm of Latino boys as uninterested in their education.

In contrast, Nancy Lopez's (2003) study on second generation youth from the Dominican Republic, the West Indies, and Haiti in New York City explores why girls of color succeed at higher rates than their male counterparts. In her study, she reveals how race and gender are stigmatized in the participants' communities and replicated in the classrooms, shaping women and men from the same ethnic group in distinct ways. She shares:

> Through the implementation of security measures, young men in particular were profiled and singled out as problematic students throughout the school … Notwithstanding the fact that men were generally more rambunctious than their female counterparts, teachers were generally less understanding of young men and were more likely to discipline them more harshly for the same infractions committed by their female counterparts. (p. 88)

Lopez claims that it is crucial to analyze the experiences in education of the children of immigrants since education still represents the most important measure of a person's social mobility. She argues that when issues of race and gender intersect, they carry with them social relations and social organizations that shape an individual's life.

Even though the above studies recognize gender differences between Latino boys and Latina girls, there is little information on the personal counterstorytelling of Latino teenage boys in school and/or how the social categories of race and gender intersect with racism and other forms of subordination by shaping Latino boys' is identities and affecting their academic achievement. Stanton-Salazar and Spina (2000) argue that when mainstream ideologies and assimilationist strategies lack a critical interrogation of "societal systems of exclusion" like racism, the resilient and "successful" turn into "model minorities," while those left behind are blamed for their choices (meritocracy) (p. 244).

Conclusion

Solórzano and Yosso (2009) argue that most of the gender studies privilege "White men, the middle and/or upper class, and heterosexuals by naming these social locations as natural or normative points of reference" (p. 134). Few research studies on Latino immigrants and U.S.-born Latinos explore the personal experiences of Latino boys only. When mainstream ethnic studies refer to gender differences on the Latino/Latina group, boys' failure in education always represents the norm. Few or no studies show Latino boys' development of resiliency to succeed academically. While utilizing CCW, most studies have focused on Latinas or Chicanas in higher education or as mothers, excluding the experiences of teenage boys in education. When academic performance statistics and traditional quantitative studies analyze Latino/Latina students under the pan-ethnic label Latino, Hispanic, or minority, their histories of resiliency and hard work are usually silenced and ignored. Although some Latino/Latina students learn to use their CCW to resist oppression in order to succeed, they are always labeled (Latino, Hispanic, minority, student of color, at risk, left behind, race to the top) as culturally deficient by the dominant group. This book should be read as an attempt to fill the necessary gap in the current literature, as it utilizes CRT/LatCrit, and Chicano/Chicana epistemologies to unveil Latino teenage boys' experiences with racism and other layers of subordination in school. It also reveals how they use their CCW to develop resiliency and a network orientation to navigate and succeed in school.

Overview of Chapters

Previous relevant studies in communities of color and education reveal how the use of a deficit-thinking model has been used in academia and teacher education programs to understand Communities of Color and education. For that reason, I challenge how some studies developed in Mexican/Latino/Chicano families and education contradict what previous ethnic studies claim about Communities of Color. I also discuss some of the most salient gender studies in Latino/Latina, Chicano/Chicana, and Mexican youth and their experiences in school. Finally, I unpack what issues related to Latino boys' educational experiences need more discussion.

Chapter II, *El Que Es Perico Donde Quiera Es Verde*, reveals how the students' counterstories unveil some of the most common barriers Latino boys cope with while trying to attain their education. In these stories, I unearth how these Latino teenage boys' problems with gangs, father's absence, gender privilege (freedom), parenting, low self-esteem, and being undocumented shape their educational experiences and personal lives. I also interrogate teachers' low expectations of Latino boys and unpack issues of a deficit-thinking model, colorblindness, meritocracy, and gender neutrality.

Chapter III, *El Que Persevera Triunfa*, explains how these Latino boys' counterstories unveil motivational factors shaped by personal motivation, family members, friends, sports, and local institutions that impact their education. While most Latino boys decide to drop out of school due to common barriers, in my study, I unveil how nine Latino teenage boys became "exceptional cases" (Garcia, 2001) and learned to build on their cultural capitals to develop resiliency and a social network support that allowed them to remain in school.

Chapter IV, *Juntos Pero No Revueltos*, unpacks Latino boys' counterstorytelling dealing with issues of *Latinidad* having different socio-economic, cultural backgrounds, and immigration experiences. This chapter explores how the participants' communal experiences with issues of heritage language, skin tone, and gender shape their identities as Latino boys and men. Finally, this chapter shows how Latino boys' definitions of *vergüenza* (shame) for being poor, undocumented, or for being labeled Hispanic or Latino affect their education and personal lives.

Chapter V, *El Muerto y El Arima'o Al Tercer Día Apesta*, analyzes how the immigration journey of some of these boys and their parents relates to their experiences in education. It explores how these boys' parents' educational and cultural backgrounds challenge the participants' academic success and upward social mobility. Finally, this chapter analyzes how the intersection of racism with issues of immigration, class, and language acquisition keep most Latino immigrant families living under a *caste minority* status that I refer as *círculo de pobreza* (circle of poverty).

Chapter VI describes how these elements contribute to the success of Latino teenage boys in education, and the limitations I encountered. I also include the challenges and implications that CRT, LatCrit, and Chicano/Chicana epistemologies may present for traditional studies and colorblind school systems, specifically among Latino/Latina students.

Note

1. For the purpose of this book, I will be using the term Latino/Latina to encompass people from Latin America or Latin American descent living in the United States. However, it is not my intention to perpetuate the assumption that Latinos/Latinas represent a homogeneous group or that there is a single identity that frames all Latin Americans in this country; on the contrary, Latinos/Latinas represent heterogeneous groups whose personal experiences of race, ethnicity, class, gender, sexual orientation, phenotype, language, and immigration vary in different contexts.

· 2 ·

EL QUE ES PERICO, DONDE QUIERA ES VERDE (A PARROT IS GREEN NO MATTER WHERE IT IS)

The continued failure of so many young men of color not only increases the likelihood that they'll end up in prison, permanently unemployed, or dead at an early age, but that our society will accept such conditions as normal. (Noguera, 2012, p. 12)

Room 155 became the nurturing space where my students and I learned to heal our experiences as Latino/Latina immigrants to this country. It was in this ESL room where our *Otherness* was not questioned, where we could cross-linguistic borders *y hablar Español* without being asked to speak only the oppressor's language. In this English as a Second Language (ESL) room my students' heritage language was valued and nurtured as a cultural springboard to learn how to navigate in two different worlds. In this basement room we freely talked about racism, immigration, parents' separation, fiestas, future goals, and frustrations. In this ESL room we met Sandra Cisneros, Pat Mora, Julia Alvarez, Francisco Jiménez, Isabel Allende, Pablo Neruda, Victor Martinez, Paul Cuadros, and many other Latino/Latina and Chicano/Chicana writers. These authors encouraged us not only to find commonalities but to create a sense of togetherness and *familia* as we unpacked our *sabidurías de vida* (life wisdom). It was in the book *A Parrot in the Oven* by Victor Martinez (1996) where character Manuel (Manny) Hernandez, a 14-year-old Mexican-American teenage boy complained about how "hot it is in the shade without knowing that all along he's sitting inside the oven" (p. 52). As a typical teenager, Manny tries to find out what it means to be a strong and respected *vato* (boy). Later, he discovers that he does not need to be in a gang to fit in. All he needs is to become more mature and to develop his own identity. Through this identity development, his alcoholic father reminds him, *El que es perico, donde quiera es verde*. Besides making reference that people (as *perico*) behave the same way regardless of their location, Manny's father tries to teach him to become a strong person and stop trusting the wrong people. Through discussing Manny's life experiences, my students and I discussed gangs, drugs, alcohol, racism, class issues, and parent-child relationships. In our room, we heard and told stories, we healed, and developed resiliency together.

Barriers to Achievement in Education

Perico, or parrot, was what Dad called me sometimes. It was from a Mexican saying about a parrot that complains how hot it is in the shade, while all along he's sitting inside an oven. People usually say this when talking about ignorant people who don't know where they're at in the world. I didn't mind it so much, actually, because Dad didn't say it because he thought I was dumb, but because I trusted everything too much, because I'd go right into the oven trusting people all the way—brains or no brains. (From *Parrot in the Oven* by Victor Martinez, 1996, pp. 51–52)

In this chapter, I analyze how these nine boys' narratives about gang affiliation, a father's absence, being a parent, low self-esteem, and immigration status affected their education and personal lives. I argue that teachers, school administrators, and parents ignore most of the social and psychological barriers that Latino boys cope with through their educational experiences. In this section, I also unearth how some Latino families allowed boys to have more freedom due to gender privilege and expectations with the idea that boys know intrinsically how to protect themselves. I argue that while having more freedom, Latino boys become more vulnerable to engage in pre-marital relationships leading them to experience fatherhood at a young age, and participate in gang activity, drugs, and crime. To corroborate with my findings and interpretations, I also include some of these boys' teachers' stories. Through their narratives and my classroom observations, I unveil how teachers' low expectations, banking method, culturally biased ideas, and gender stereotypes perpetuate colorblindness and a deficit-thinking model in education that sees minorities of color as culturally deficient (Valencia, 2010), promoting inequity in this underrepresented group. Finally, I explore how through the development of a network support, built upon their community cultural wealth, these nine Latino boys became resilient and continued with their education.

Gangs

> The cop checked us out, trying to assemble our *movida* as he studied and memorized our faces. He could have stopped us, but it was only a little after seven, not yet dark, and the night was going to get scary in about two hours. He probably figured why waste my time with a couple of young *burros* like us. (From *Buried Onions* by Gary Soto, 2006, p. 83)

When I started teaching in the Southeast in 1999, gang-related problems were big issues. It was common to see Latino boys and sometimes girls being arrested or taken to jail for bringing drugs or weapons to school, or for having gang initiation fights at the mall or behind the church close to campus. When I began my teaching job at a different high school in the same county, a Latino gang member told me: "You came here to ruin everything." Some teachers and students felt intimidated by certain Latino boys who would hang out around the hall, making it almost impossible to walk through the area. Once, I reported a student for having a gang sign on a cross; he was then sent to In-School-Suspension (ISS). Then next day, I realized my car was keyed. Gangs were (and still are) a big social problem in this community.

Before I got my teaching job in this high school in 2002, a local Latina pastor friend of mine warned me about a community meeting held by the local police and the school district to discuss gang prevention issues in which they were targeting young males of color. Since there was a lot of misinformation and racial tension about Latino/Latina immigrants in the community, I felt it was my responsibility—as an educator, community leader, and freelance writer for a Latino newspaper—to be part of this meeting.

When I arrived, to my surprise the school auditorium where the meeting was held was full of white people, a few African American parents, and the Latina pastor with her congregation. I was in shock when I realized that the police department had on display some posters showing the *homies* (cartoons and figures based upon Chicano/Chicana characters and life styles) which were very popular among my Latino/Latina students. Wrongly, the police department used those posters for people to profile Latino/Latina youth in loose clothing as gang members. Before the meeting started, I decided to go ahead and talk to the special guest, a white man who came to teach the participants how to identify gang-related signs and behavioral patterns. During my conversation, I asked the speaker to not perpetuate stereotypes against Latinos since many of us were already not welcomed in the community. Even though he never mentioned Latinos/Latinas as gang members, the posters, pictures, and videos shown during the conference portrayed mostly men of color as gangsters. Also, the fact that there was a lot tension in the community due to the new immigrants was evident through racist letters to the editor published in the only local newspaper. It perpetuated the idea that Latino/Latina immigrants represented a social threat for the community and the school system.

Over the years, gang-related problems changed both in the community and in the school system. This high school, for example, had an administrator in charge of the school discipline whose job was to punish or expel students, with a large number of them being Latino and Black boys. Rios (2011) argues that when young men are exposed to patterns of punishment, it has the potential to increase their decisions to commit crime and engage in violence. I witnessed how many of these young boys became disrespectful to this school administrator, especially when they were ridiculed in front of their peers and teachers. Many of them were sent to in-school-suspension (ISS), out-of-school suspension (OSS), and others decided to quit school. Even though teachers and school administrators agreed that these boys got in trouble for breaking school norms, these students, their parents, and some concerned community leaders, including myself, agreed that their ethnicity and gender made them more vulnerable to punishment and stereotypes than other boys in the school.

Alex and Luis had been in the U.S. school system longer than the other participants in my study and both had overcome more social and personal barriers than the rest. They were born in this country, raised by single parents, and struggled to complete their senior year. Both had part-time jobs at fast food restaurants after school and on weekends. By the end of the first interview with Alex, I reminded him that I was interested in Latino teenage boys' experiences in school. I asked him if he wanted me to include something else as part of my study. He mentioned that I needed to include issues of gangs in schools. I let him run the conversation. Alex said:

> Gangs because I came from Los Angeles and when I was there, I was still a kid, but I saw … my oldest brothers like nine years older than me … and then the second one is five years older, so they grew up with it, so they brought it down here and well my dad left when I was eight. I think I was like in a fourth grade, so going into middle

school, my brothers ... that are all that I saw [gang activity]. Is not that I got peer pressure to do anything 'cause it was my decision that got [me] into a gang; started hanging around bad people and ... quickly turned it around ... talked to myself that it's not a good—like, it won't be a good life. I try to do well in school. I try everything I do out of school to leave it outside. When I come to school, I try to keep my grades up. My goal was to graduate; after that I focus on going to college.

Alex's counterstory on gang affiliation showed how he became a victim of his own environment. Raised by a single parent, who probably worked long hours or had more than one job to support the family, and having older brothers as negative role models shaped Alex's identity as a Latino boy who eventually became a gang member.

During our first group conversations, I wanted to engage these boys in a dialogue to unpack Alex's stories on gangs. For that, I shared with them my preliminary analysis based on their first conversations and my observations. I mentioned that based on my experience as a teacher, other research studies, and my interpretations, being affiliated with gangs was one of the reasons Latino boys drop out of school. As a result, some of these boys did not agree with my interpretations. Luis argued that gangs used to be a big problem at school and that maybe in the past students used to drop out because of gang affiliation, but not anymore. Pedro agreed but also mentioned how his father prevented him from joining a gang. He said:

I remember when I was in middle school there was a lot of gang activity. My dad was always "that stupid; that's a waste of time." Like that's just dumb. You should be in school, studying and getting a good job and not worrying about drugs and all that stuff. And I didn't. I didn't really think about gangs. No one ever asked me to join a gang.

It is clear that Pedro's father's influence and awareness about gangs in school discouraged him from joining one. While using words such as "stupid" and "dumb," Pedro's father encouraged him to make smart choices in life. His father also reminded him about the real purpose of attending school: to get an education and a better future.

At this point, Alex was the only participant who decided to talk about gang affiliation. Most of the other boys referred to it as something that happened in middle school while some others never heard about it. However, during the second face-to-face interviews, most of the boys like Pedro shared how their parents, relatives, and close friends talked to them about avoiding gang-related activities. José and Juan shared how through their relatives' (cousins and uncles) and brothers' gang affiliation and negative outcomes, their parents taught them about gang problems. I discuss more about what Juan learned from his brother's experience with gangs later in this study. Most of these boys chose to play sports or to join other extra-curricular activities at school or at local institutions. Like many scholars, Garcia (2001) agrees that when schools invest in students' behaviors and their involvement and interest in school-related activities, it improves student academic achievement and engagement. In this study, I learned that being engaged in sports and other community activities prevented some of these boys from joining gangs.

When Alex and I met to have our second conversation, I decided to ask him more specific questions about his gang affiliation. I asked him if gangs were still common. He shared that gangs were rare in school. He said that there were still gangs, but not as bad as it used to be. He stated that some of the boys who used to be in the same gang did not talk to each other anymore; "They don't like each other anymore like when we used to hang out a lot." Later, I shared how through my experience as a teacher, I saw boys being labeled gang members because of having tattoos, or wearing a bandana or certain colors. I also noticed Alex had some tattoos on his arm, chest, and fingers.

R.V.:	Have people questioned the tattoos you have on your skin?
Alex:	Uhuh, but is nothing bad. [showing it to me] the California state, and I have one here that says "Have Faith." Because it means something to me. I always have to keep my faith and keep going even if I am still struggling.
R.V.:	What about the dots?
Alex:	Oh, oh, those are gang related.
R.V.:	Is that Latin King?
Alex:	Uhuh.
R.V.:	Tell me about it.
Alex:	They just mean … they mean like five points and they mean obedience, honesty, loyalty, righteousness, and honor.
R.V.:	What does that mean to you?
Alex:	Well, I was more into it when I was smaller, fourteen; thirteen … 'cause I guess that was the rebel stage.
R.V.:	There's also a crown there. [Latin King symbol.]
Alex:	Yeah, … [it's] a Latin King symbol but I was more into it when I was little.
R.V.:	Not anymore?
Alex:	No … Back then … everything has calmed down … like when I started as freshman there was a lot of that here.

R.V.:   One of my former students told me you can never get out of that once
           you get in.
Alex: I guess you can stop ... socializing and all that but ... mostly every-
           body has ... leads dots somewhere ... I mean you can stop socializing.
           I mean they still know who you are but you are no longer like ... get
           around [as a part of the gang]. A lot of people judge what they see.
R.V.:   Have you experienced that?
Alex: Yeah, a lot of people, people saw me and judged me like wrong or
           something, but I try now to focus on school.

Even though Alex mentioned that he was not an active gang member he also corroborated what my former students had already told me about gang affiliation. Most of the time, gang members are taught that once they join a gang they cannot step out. He also recognized that being in a gang was not a good choice, and that he did it when he was younger, as part of his teenage phase. He explained that whatever he did was outside the school building. It seemed to me that he still identified himself as a Latin King. He was also aware that people questioned his gang affiliation because of his tattoos; how-ever, he also wanted both worlds—to be a part of the gang and to succeed in school in order to become a role model for others and to make his mother and siblings feel proud of him. He said, "I wanna see myself succeed. I wanna see myself ... I wanna tell somebody when I am older. Yeah, I've been through that, I've done that, been through that. I've gone through those obstacles, and I still succeeded." Alex became what Prudence Carter (2005) refers to as a "cultural straddler." He developed the skills to navigate two worlds: school expectations and his gang affiliation. Unfortunately, after my last interview with Alex, some teachers shared with me their concerns about his ability to graduate since he had missed so many days of school. Although he tried to work hard, his long-working hours deterred him from attending school regularly.

Sadly, in my years of teaching I witnessed many Latino boys and a few girls join gangs, get in trouble in school and the community, use drugs, and finally drop out of school. Even though most of these boys think about gangs as a thing of the past, in my work as a teacher I witnessed gang affiliation and recruitment still occurring in this community. Gang members have learned to use different venues (social media) to reach out to these young boys and girls. In order to fit in or to find a sense of belonging, some Latino/Latina teenagers have no choice but to join gangs where they feel accepted as *familia*. Suárez-Orozco and Suárez-Orozco (2001) posit, "Gangs appear to provide an ini-tial exhilarating lifestyle—one that lies in sharp contrast to that provided by schools, which they view as not only uninspiring but also as rejecting them" (p. 112). When some Latino boys lack a positive and caring adult male role model within their families and school that can help them understand life and school obstacles; they usually find those models somewhere else, even when those individuals represent a negative influence in their lives.

Fatherless

> Indio missed his father; the emptiness, the vacancy, in his home and in his heart was growing bigger and bigger with each day. It consumed him and plagued every waking moment of his young life … He begged his mother to let him go to the United States to be reunited with his father. (From *A Home on the Field* by Paul Cuadros, 2006 p. 202)

During the conversations, these boys agreed that having a male figure as a positive role model influenced their lives. Although most of them suggested that boys need a father figure that they can look up to, someone who can support and motivate them to do well in life, they also acknowledged that their mothers were doing their best by raising them as single parents. I learned that four of these boys did not have fathers at home.

Alex shared how much he missed not having his father around, but he also shared how his mother tried to teach him how to behave as "a good boy." Still, he mentioned how being fatherless affected him during his childhood and adolescence. He said:

> I guess that when my dad left I didn't have anybody to look up to, just my mom, so she had to be the male role model … like when I was ten, eleven, twelve, she used to tell me how to treat my girlfriends right, right things from wrong things, telling me basically what a father would tell a grown child.

It is important to highlight that when boys do not have male adults at home or school as positive role model figures, they tend to find them in the streets. Unfortunately, most of those role models represent a negative influence on most boys. Pedro's counterstory about his father's absence served as an example of how some Latino boys miss having their fathers' presence around them. He shared that while he was growing up his father spent most of the time on the road, working as a truck driver, so they hardly spent time together: "I don't get to see him a lot, like even when I was growing up [I] did not get to see him a lot." During the second interview I discovered that Pedro's parents had recently divorced. He said,

They stopped getting along. They started fighting. We moved and we sold our house and we moved and then my dad since he was never there, he works then. I hardly see him before that. Now I see him less. I think I only see him twice a year; twice this year.

Even though Pedro was very quiet, his parents' divorce and teenage sister's pregnancy influenced his studies. When I asked him if his parents' divorce affected him, he said, "Kinda. I didn't grow up with a dad. Kinda he never taught me useful stuff. I kinda learned everything on my own or from my friends, certain things." Moreover, Pedro learned how to use his social and navigational capital and sports as an outlet to forget about his family problems. When I asked him if he had ever thought about dropping out of school, he stated, "No because I think it's dumb, like a lot of people like why waste eleven or twelve years of your life and just drop out. Instead go to college or go and do something with your life." Pedro's comments about staying in school also showed how he was making use of his familial and aspirational capital, and how he developed his own social and navigational networks to stay in school. Stanton-Salazar and Spina (2000) state that when low-income racial youth develops resiliency as a network-based action, it leads the individual to participate in multiple "socio-cultural worlds and institutional domains," allowing social mobility (p. 241). Joining different sports after school not only helped Pedro escape from his family problems for a while, but it also helped him navigate and develop a social network among his peers and coaches, allowing him to stay out of trouble and to remain in school.

During the first conversation, I shared how my preliminary analysis showed that the absence of the father figure due to parents' separation affected Latino boys' motivation toward schooling and their self-esteem. It allowed these boys to unpack their ideas about not having a father figure at home.

Alex:	is just like with the absence of the father figure like who's gonna show you, who's gonna motivate you to … that part of your life is gonna be gone you know; is like your mom has to be your mom and your dad.
Carlos:	I disagree with the parents' divorce because my parents divorced since I was 6 years old and my father lives in New Jersey and I live in _____ and I still keep in touch with my father. It affects me because my father pushes me every day, every night I talk to him, he tells me to move forward like "how are you doing in school," he calls school all the way from New Jersey to make sure I get tutoring to make sure I get all the help I need.
Alex:	But you think it will be different if he were here with you, living with you?
Carlos:	No because I still keep in touch with him and talk to him all the time.

Carlos's comments show how he does not feel his father's physical absence affects him since he calls him and checks on his studies. It is important to note that due to immigration, most Latino parents leave their children, especially boys, back home, forming psychological scars. Some fathers keep supporting their children's education and well-being by calling or sending money back home. Even though they are not there physically, often there is still a father-son relationship and love. Some other fathers forget about their families back home and start new families in this country, making it difficult for mothers and relatives to raise boys without a father figure. In some cases, the grandfather or uncles play a dad's role. Cammarota (2008) posits that Latina mothers usually raise their families on their own since male-dominated society accepts the state of men's indifference to raise their own children. In my study, four of these boys did not have a positive relationship with their fathers. Alex, who missed having his father as a positive role model while growing up, explained how his father's absence shaped his childhood and bad decisions in life. Juan always mentioned his father as a careless person who let his older brother play the father's role in the house. Likewise, Raúl mentioned that moving with his father during his adolescence was a very bad experience since his father did not have the patience to take care of him and his siblings. Finally, Pedro mentioned how much time his father spent at work during his childhood and that he almost never saw him at home. His mother took his father's role once they separated.

Rios (2011) posits, "Gender is one of the processes in which the criminal justice system and the youth control complex are involved in the production of criminalization, social exclusion, and racial inequality" (p. 141). Although my study explores how these Latino teenage boys learn to use their cultural capital to develop resilience and a network support to remain in school, studies suggest that when Latino boys do not find male role models at home or at any other institution, like the school, they are more likely to become victims of a street sub-culture (gangs). Gangs provide them with damaging messages about masculinity, pushing them to develop resistant and violent patterns as part of a hypermasculinity expected by the dominant society and school and then used to marginalize them. In Rios (2011), Angela Harris defines hypermasculinity as "exaggerated exhibition of physical strength and personal aggression" (p. 130). Others see this hypermasculintiy as an answer to "a gender threat expressed through physical and sexual domination of others" (p. 130). Some Latino boys are brought up with the assumption that because of their gender, they have to have more freedom than girls in order to prepare them to be strong and future householders. Giving Latino boys freedom also leads them to experience pre-marital sex, young parenting, alcohol, and drugs, which makes them even more vulnerable to stereotyping and gender discrimination, worsening their chances to remain in school.

"Boys Will Be Boys" Freedom

> Immigrant families are often caught in powerful and contradicting social currents, which result in both radical change and regidification. In the realm of gender relations, many of the paradoxes created by immigration appear with clarity and force. (Suárez-Orozco & Suárez-Orozco, 2001, p. 77)

One of the biggest obstacles Latino boys face in school is the fact that they cannot make use of the freedom they are entitled to as boys in their own communities. When boys are not allowed to make use of that freedom in school, they may become defiant and resistant, developing oppositional identities against teachers and school authorities. Some others misinterpret their freedom and engage in teen sexual activities, representing a significant barrier in their education and personal lives. I argue that these types of gender expectations make Latino boys more vulnerable to becoming teenage parents and/ or to get involved in other social problems with negative consequences.

During the first conversations I asked the students why boys were given more freedom by their parents than girls. Most of their comments reemphasized issues of gender heteronormativity and social constructs about Latino boys and men, that they know how to protect themselves because they are stronger and smarter than girls. Luis said, "Parents think that girls are gonna end up doing something bad … and … like getting pregnant or something." In this book I learned that because they are boys, parents trust them more or because of the fact that boys cannot get pregnant there are less chances that they will get in trouble. Likewise, Carlos described girls as weak and less trustworthy than boys:

> I believe it's true because I notice it a lot. I think parents are scared more about girls being with other guys and they can't really defend themselves 'cause majority of girls are more feminine than guys … guys are stronger … they know how to take care of themselves [better] than girls … that's what I think … and that's why parents trust the guys [to] be by themselves [more] than girls.

Pedro explained how his father trusted him more for being the only boy at home. Again, there is an assumption that because some boys are physically bigger than girls, they are also strong enough to make the right choices and to protect themselves. During the conversation, Pedro added that as a teenage boy he was also aware of his vulnerability of getting a girl pregnant; however, as a boy it is more acceptable to have sex than girls. He said:

> I understand because my parents, my dad is always strict with my sisters but as for me they trust me more because I'm a boy and I can't get pregnant but at the same time they worry about me getting a girl pregnant so I can see where they're coming from. Parents are afraid that girls can get pregnant, but a boy can get someone else pregnant. I think that's why Latino boys get more freedom than girls.

Rios (2011) argues, "To be assigned "real man" status by relevant others and institutions, men must pass multiple litmus tests among peers, family, and institutions" (p. 131). Unfortunately, those Latino boys who decide to pass those tests while having pre-marital sex do so with Latina girls who are usually younger and very naïve about the consequences of teenage pregnancy and parenting. Parents avoid having honest conversations about sexuality with girls, wrongly assuming that if they talk about it, girls will do it earlier than expected. Even when parents do talk to girls about dating and pre-marital sex, there is a sense of fear, especially if parents had their own children at young age.

Alex shared how he enjoyed his freedom just for being a boy; his mom assumed that he could take care of himself. Instead, his older sisters had to wait until they became teenagers to obtain some type of freedom. While they were younger, his sisters did not know how to take care of themselves. He said:

> I think because they're more protective of girls, like they know what ... bad things will happen to ... like they're girls, but guys, they know that when we hit certain age, we can basically defend ourselves and be on at least try to be responsible of what we do ... like my mom, she lets my sisters go out. She lets them go out since they were like 16 or 17 because she trusts my sisters. How with me and my brothers, she lets us go out since like around age 2.

The boys agreed that their parents overprotect the girls because they fear they might get pregnant or do something wrong. They felt that parents trust boys more than girls. The fact that Latino boys are given more freedom at home, assuming they can learn about life to be able to solve problems, become strong, and be future household providers leads them to develop an expected hypermasculinity. Conchas and Vigil (2012) argue that even though adolescents experience some "developmental phases" such as "hormonal and physical transformations, these phases depend on the eco-cultural system the person lives in—such as home, school, or the streets and the role models found therein" (p. 17). They claim, "the streets in high-poverty neighborhoods offer different obstacles and dictate various options to skew such phases and normal activities" (p. 17). Since boys get to experience more freedom than girls, they are more exposed to activities that many consider as normal within their communities, such as drinking alcohol, taking drugs, or having pre-marital sex, making them vulnerable to problems with the law, unplanned parenting, and stereotypes. I argue that most Latino parents give more freedom to boys, assuming that they know how to protect themselves; however, the constant pressure they get from peers, the media, and society at large, push them to prove their manhood by making bad choices in life.

Parenting

If you're a teenager, the whole world hates you. If you're a pregnant teenager, people think you should be burned at the stake. I'm a Mexican, pregnant sixteen-year-old. So shoot me and get it over with. (From *Seedfolks* by Paul Fleischman, 2002, p. 66)

During my years of teaching in public schools in this country, I witnessed how often Latino boys were obliged to interrupt their education once they realized they were becoming parents. Regardless of their socio-economic situation, immigration status, or academic performance, most of these boys ended up finding jobs in local factories, landscaping, or fast-food restaurants. Due to lack of support at home and school, most of them realized that obtaining a high school diploma was not their priority; making money to support their new families was their responsibility.

Luis was the only student in my book who was a parent. Although Luis shared how his son became part of his motivation for being in school, I decided to ask him more in-depth questions about his role and responsibility as a young father. During the first focus group, I shared that in my book I claimed that one of the barriers that leads Latino teenage boys to drop out of school occurs when they become young parents. Luis disagreed with my comments and said, "I have a kid and it doesn't mean that I am gonna drop out of school and leave … just 'cause I have a kid." I reminded him that his point was valid and well taken, but I also made him aware that he represented an exception to the rule and that was one of the reasons why his participation in my book was so important, so others could hear and learn from his experience as a young father. I let him know that in my years of teaching I had seen how often Latino boys who became parents decided to leave the school in order to find a job to support their new families.

R.V.:	How old is your child now?
Luis:	He's two years and two months. We had a little get together for his first year. He turned two in October.
R.V.:	How old were you when you had the baby?
Luis:	When I first found out … [thinking]. When I first had him, I was sixteen.
R.V.:	Did you want to be a father?
Luis:	No, but I don't regret it now.
R.V.:	Did your father talk to you about sex and what could happen?
Luis:	Not really, he just told me to be careful whenever … I did stuff. He told me to protect me, be careful.
R.V.:	Do you think that if your father had talked to you about safe sex, it wouldn't have happened?
Luis:	Maybe but … it just [thinking]. It was an accident.
R.V.:	Are you still together with the child's mom?
Luis:	Yes.
R.V.:	How has your life changed compared to somebody who has no children?
Luis:	I have to work and pay stuff. I have to give up some things. I cannot go and take off like I used to do before like I used to go on vacation with my dad's friends.
R.V.:	Do you think you have to be responsible now because you have a child?
Luis:	I think I have matured a little more. I would probably be thinking about partying too, but … it doesn't interest me as much.
R.V.:	Do you see yourself moving in with your child's mother?
Luis:	Maybe later on, not right now. I don't know; I don't see myself taking the whole responsibility of living with someone. For right now it's too much.
R.V.:	So she lives with her mom and you live with your dad. Are you working now?
Luis:	Yes. Well, now _____ Pizza. I started working back at the end of November. I mean I didn't have to go back but is just extra money. My dad is helping out a lot.
R.V.:	What were your parents' reactions when they knew you were gonna be a father?
Luis:	My dad was kinda of mad first, but then he kinda got over it. My mom was very supportive. She told me that if I knew what I had got into, I had to take the whole responsibility of it and my actions. And if I needed something, she would help me out. And my dad later on told me the same thing but at first he was mad.
R.V.:	How did you feel when you knew you were gonna be a father?
Luis:	I was scared. I was scared. It's hard to hear that.

Having a familial support (capital) allowed Luis to remain in school; however, his fatherhood responsibilities pushed him to find a part-time job to support his son and girlfriend. This reinforces the idea of *familia es familia* (family is family) no matter the circumstances. *Familia* always comes first.

Like Alex, Luis's school attendance was very poor when I finished our conversations. Although he learned to navigate and to develop a social network at school, his academic performance had put him in danger of not getting a high school diploma. It is important to note that I limited the number of students who were in school at the time; therefore, students who dropped out due, at least in part, to being parents would not be represented in my book. Being a gang member, not having a male role model, or becoming a father might represent physical barriers many Latino boys have to face, but what happens when their battles are invisible to others? What happens when a Latino boy is afraid to be ridiculed or questioned for not fitting a societal mold?

Low Self-Esteem

> I dropped out of high school and moved out of my house because it was scary there. My stepfather drank from the time he got home until the time everything funny on television became news or talk shows ... I had been lonely in high school. From my seat in Biology, I had paid more attention to the weather reflected in the windows than to the frogs with their legs in the air. (From *Jesse* by Gary Soto, 1994, pp. 1–2)

Due to the fact that dominant constructions of masculinity in both white U.S. culture and Latino culture promote the idea that men should always be strong and never admit sadness or lack of confidence, Latino boys rarely externalize signs of depression or low self-esteem. Some of them are afraid to become victims of bullying or harassment for showing weakness in front of their peers. In addition, in the school setting a lack of understanding and caring about Latino boys' personal and familial problems leads teachers and school administrators to assume that Latino boys' misbehavior and lack of motivation at school are mostly associated with being resistant or with being culturally deficient.

Although Juan's academic performance made him be seen by others as a smart and happy Latino teenage boy, in this study he shared how much he suffered internally. Since my first interview, he shared how much he disliked his parents for not being good to him. He always argued that his father let his oldest brother lead the family. His oldest brother then tried to force Juan to work around the house, more than should be his share. Juan argued that his brother was very demanding and dominant. He shared that once the landlord asked his older brother to clean one of the empty apartments. Instead, Juan's brother, using profane language and insults, demanded that Juan clean out one of the apartments for him. For that reason, he left his parents' house and moved in with his adult friends Rosa and Sarah. Rosa was a Latina woman who used to work at the local library as a librarian and Sarah, a white woman, was Rosa's friend. They both supported him when he decided to focus on his studies to show himself and others that he would accomplish his goals of getting good grades in order to attend college. Later in this study I unveil how Rosa and Sarah motivated Juan to remain in school.

Before having the second focus group meeting, I asked Juan if he would be willing to speak to me individually. In the first focus group Juan did not share much, so I decided to have a separate interview with him to make sure I could hear his stories. I noticed that during the first focus group, Juan remained silent after Luis's comments about undocumented students. As a joke, Luis mentioned that some undocumented students tried to behave white to fit in. He continued saying that he was an American citizen but did not have to act white. Luis's comments made Juan feel uncomfortable.

While I was waiting to meet with Juan, it surprised me when some teachers asked me to talk to him; they were worried because he was not doing well. I wanted to better understand Juan's situation at school. During our conversation, I asked him if he had learned any lessons about life from his parents and he said no. I asked him how he learned to deal with life issues. He said, "Just from experiences I had in the past." He told me that the only adults around him were Rosa and Sarah, but Rosa had moved back to California and Sarah was always working; so basically he had nobody around. He then revealed that for that reason, he had tried to commit suicide. It seemed to me that he missed Rosa's physical presence. He said, "It was like I was feeling depressed and usually when I am feeling depressed I like doing stupid stuff. I wanted to get a pill overdose or stab myself; why not?" Juan's lack of parental support and low self-esteem pushed him to feel depressed and to think about committing suicide. It is important to note that during my observations, I witnessed how Juan almost never interacted with other boys. Instead, he preferred to work by himself and always referred to the other boys as being "stupid" or "dumb" for not paying attention or for asking irrelevant questions in class. Most of the time I observed that Juan interacted with girls, especially white girls. Even though Juan spoke English fluently, he did not fit within the dominant culture because of his ethnicity, dark skin, and immigration status. Valenzuela (1999) shares that immigrant youth suffer depression in their efforts toward a "rapid cultural assimilation" (p. 93). She argues that this results in "maladjustment," which leads them to be marginalized "not only with respect to the academic mainstream, but also in relation to their family's social identity" (p. 93). Although Juan was born in Mexico, he was brought up in the U.S. speaking only English and embracing the U.S. culture as the only one he knew. However, as a teenager, Juan's internal conflict within his own ethnic group and assimilation of a white American culture led him to experience isolation, "maladjustment." I witnessed how his own peers made fun of him for pretending to be "white" although everybody knew that he was in the country illegally.

Although Juan experienced marginalization for being a Mexican boy with dark skin and undocumented, he challenged school and social norms. Juan seemed to have a good rapport with most teachers, but none of them were aware of his internal battles. Amazingly, Juan always found that inner light of encouragement and hope to overcome his family and self-esteem struggles. Juan's counterstory proved how he used his network orientation, by moving in with Rosa and Sarah, which allowed him to achieve academic success. Even though he did not live with his parents and siblings, he developed a social network of support from his friends, Rosa and Sarah, and a local institution (the library) to work hard in order to stay in school. He said:

> That's why I used to go to the library. Like when they saw my report card and they saw a B and like I know you can do better. Like we believe in you and they took me to do stuff. Like Ms. Daisy [pseudonym, a librarian] before she died. She took me to eat; she bought me clothes. She bought me a tux for the Beta Club initiation in seventh grade and just that little stuff helps, makes me believe in myself.

Even though he experienced family and personal struggles, he tried to overcome those obstacles by focusing on his studies. Using his parents' lack of support and his siblings' lived experiences in school, Juan developed his own resiliency by breaking a family cycle of failure. Juan said, "I am doing good. Every teacher that I had says that I am a good student and that's not gonna ... I am not gonna be like my brothers, I am different. And that's how that's gonna be."

During my experience as a teacher, I also witnessed some Latino boys experiencing low self-esteem due to acculturation and/or family problems. Even though some of them decided to drop out of school, some others, like Juan, decided to develop a network orientation at school or in their communities that allowed them to experience resiliency to stay in school. Most of my former Latino students dropped out of school due to internal problems associated with their self-esteem and lack of support that could keep them in school. Some of them associated their low self-esteem as a part of their immigration status. Some of them realized that they could not pursue higher education in this country because they were undocumented. However, only a few of them, like some of the boys in my study, became resilient and continued with their education regardless of their immigration status.

Undocumented

> During the conversation her father asked me what my nationality was.
> "Why did he ask you?" I said, recalling the time I met Peggy's parents.
> "He wanted to know where the name *Jimenez* came from. I told him."
> "You didn't tell him."
> "No, I didn't tell him I was born in Mexico," he said, anticipating the question. "But when I said I was Mexican there was dead silence. After a while he continued talking but they seemed uncomfortable and less friendly." (From *Breaking Through* by Francisco Jiménez, 2001, p. 107)

Being undocumented has always been the toughest barrier for Latino/Latina immigrant students, especially when considering college while in high school. Even those who work hard to challenge stereotypes and conform to the dominant culture realize that because of their lack of legal documentation, they are not allowed to attend college in this country. Although some colleges and universities have opened their doors to undocumented immigrants, having to pay out-of-state tuition fees without any type of federal loans or scholarships leaves most undocumented students with the understanding that pursuing a higher education is an unaffordable dream. Instead, most of them who graduate from high school end up working in low wage jobs and eventually start having their own families. Juan's academic performance showed his aspirations to pursue higher education and become a professional; however, his immigration status in this country represented yet another of the barriers most undocumented students, like Juan, too often face when they reach high school. He said, "Sometimes because we are Latinos and we don't have papers sometimes people assume we are not gonna get out of high school and do something with our lives." Juan's comments show how some undocumented students decide to challenge others' low expectations and negative labeling about Latino/Latina students' immigration status. Besides struggling with his cultural identity and family problems, Juan had to face people's assumptions about him for being an undocumented student. Likewise, José shared not being able to attend college in this country because of his legal status. He said:

> When they [colleges or universities] reject me for not having papers because I know this guy, he went to _____ High School and he used to play for the YMCA and he's already a good player and then some of the colleges went to see his game in _____ because there was a tournament and they saw him playing because he plays really good. And then one of the colleges they wanted him to play in one the colleges and *le iban a dar una beca para que jugara* (he was about to get a scholarship for him to play) and the first question, he was all happy and stuff *y le preguntaron que sí tenía papeles y dijo que no, entonces los del* college *na'mas lo agarraron y se fueron* (and he was asked if he had papers and he said no, then people from college walked away). Then he felt like crying and stuff. *Así me ha pasado me han mandado becas y todo* (that has already happened to me, I have received scholarship offers and everything), that's my fear, *que me hagan así* (that it happens to me) for not having papers.

Even though José was aware that his biggest barrier was not being able to get a sponsor or a scholarship to attend college, he developed resiliency as a result of his network orientation to remain in school, hoping that someone might help him fulfill his dream of playing professional soccer at a college or university in this country. Stanton-Salazar and Spina (2000) share that "Long-term development of resiliency in minority youth and young adults is synonymous with the development of a network structure" (p. 245). Although José was aware that because of his immigration status in this country he might not be able to attend college and accomplish his dream of becoming a professional soccer player, he learned to use his cultural capitals to remain in school.

Juan and José were the only undocumented participants in this study. The fact that they learned how to use the cultural capitals within their community cultural wealth to develop their own network allowed them to remain in school. It is important to note that their network structure did not occur in the classroom but on the field playing sports and at the local library. This network structure helped them to develop resiliency to work hard in school regardless of their uncertain future as higher education students.

Teachers' Low Expectations

> The concern that immigrant children *"cannot"* or *"will not"* assimilate to mainstream American culture are two sides of a single coin that are invoked sometimes separately and sometimes concurrently. The idea that the children of immigrants *cannot* be

assimilated is based partly on the assumption that they "*quality*" of today's immigrants is somehow below the quality of immigrant from previous eras. While "old immigrants" are celebrated, new immigrants are seen as falling short. (Suárez-Orozco & Suárez-Orozco, 2001, pp. 49–50)

In my last two years of teaching in this high school, I was asked to co-teach some academic subjects. Even though I disliked this idea, I gained more experience as a teacher since I met and supported many other students. I sometimes felt challenged teaching content-area curriculum but also pleased because it also gave me the opportunity to be a good role model for other students, especially my ESL and other Latino/Latina students. As a co-teacher, I also witnessed how many students experienced teachers' low expectations, leading them to be disengaged and unmotivated while trying to obtain a high school diploma. As a scholar and man of color, I felt the oppression that many teenage students experience in school, leading them to choose between invisibility (conformity) or resistance (vulnerability). What follows are notes from my field journal from a math class I observed while conducting my research data.

As the teacher is telling students what is written on the board, the class copies the information from the board. There is an essential question and she reminds students about it. Students are quietly copying from the board. José takes notes from the Smart Board. The rest of students look bored. José yawns and has a side-conversation with a Latina girl next to him. The teacher keeps lecturing the unit and reminds students that the information is in their notes and that if they missed class they need to copy the notes from the board. Some students take notes and some others do not. The only Black girl, who is seated by herself, is having a soft drink. A Latino boy at José's table puts his head down. The class is totally quiet listening to the teacher's lecture. The Latino boy next to José does not take notes at all. He is just there. The teacher encourages the only white boy to take notes. José decides to take notes now.

The teacher switches gears and plays a video documentary. As the students watch it, the teacher explains how amino acids work in the system. The Black girl puts her head down. The phone rings and a student is called to the phone. The Latino boy at José's table looks bored. José says something to the Latina girl next to him. He keeps watching the video. Then he decides to have a side conversation with the bored boy. José rubs his eyes and folds his hands. The teacher tells the class they will work on their web quest. The students pull out their laptops.

Even though these Latino boys decided to conform and do what they were asked in the classroom, they were consciously aware of how teachers' expectations were associated to the type of assignments they were given. Listening to these boys counterstories about their classroom assignments being less challenging and engaging encouraged me to spend more time observing how their comments aligned or challenged what the teachers shared about Latino boys in education.

Before the first semester observation of Pedro's English class, the teacher, Ms. Dixon, warned me that it was the worst class she had ever had and that some students should not have been placed in her honors class. Most of the students in her class were African American and Latino/Latina students. Having previously co-taught with Ms. Dixon, I knew that she generally struggled with classroom management. During the observation, her classroom environment was chaotic. Most students were logged onto their laptops, having side conversations, or texting, while Ms. Dixon was trying to review some answers to assigned homework. Even though the class consisted mainly of students of color, they still segregated themselves. African American students and Latino students each sat in distinct corners, and a small group of white students sat in the middle. When I held the second interview with Pedro, I mentioned his Honors English class with Ms. Dixon and he commented:

> I don't feel like I am learning anything. Just making me read a book and that's it. And answer questions from it. I am pretty sure a little kid can do that. I've been doing it from elementary school, reading books and answering questions. Is not really anything different. It feels like a regular class to be honest, kinda, except when she asks us to write since she wants us to write more. But I feel it's a little bit hard to write an extra more … like you don't learn anything useful. You just learn the basic stuff. She asks us to write and she expects us to know it and she doesn't go over how to write stuff … she gives us an assignment on *Moodle* and she expects to turn it in and that's it. That's the grade for today.

It is clear from Pedro's comments that he felt the teacher's expectations were too low. He did not feel challenged enough by the type of assignments his teacher gave him, especially since he was in an honors class.

As with Pedro's class, my observation of Alex's computer course unveils what happens when students are not challenged enough in the classroom. Instead of truly learning, most of them decide to conform, and to experience invisibility; others choose to listen to music or do busy work. This teacher-student communication gap leads some teachers to accept this compliant behavior as good behavior; while for some students, the compliant behavior is considered boring and less challenging.

> Alex looks bored. The teacher started talking about the grades since it's almost the end of the second six weeks. Alex is spacing out now. He is quietly looking at the

teacher. Students do not look engaged; a few of them are paying attention and others are not. The teacher asked who was absent on Tuesday.

The teacher is back, gives some papers to some students, and tells them what to do next. Alex stares at the teacher. Then he stares at me. His eyes look tired. I think he is cold too. He's waiting for the answers. He keeps filling in the words on the handouts. He hardly talks to anybody. The teacher has not talked to Alex at all since I entered the room.

Alex is checking his cellphone, probably searching for more music. He yawns now and looks down. I realize that Alex has been searching for some music on his cellphone since I started my observation. He hides it behind the computer tower. He continues writing, talking to his friend, and listening to music.

As I reviewed the boys' and teachers' interviews and classroom observations, I realized that there was a definite communication gap between teachers' expectations and students' motivations to learn. Valenzuela (1999) argues "a mutual sense of alienation evolves when teachers and students hold different understandings about school" (p. 62). The participants shared that they felt bored and unmotivated in the classroom since teachers tended to lecture, give them handouts, or require busy work on their computers. These boys agreed that their job was to take notes and to submit assignments on the computer. Most of them agreed that their classes consisted of taking notes from slides, filling out handouts, or submitting them. Some others agreed that their classes were boring since they already knew the content. Alex said this about his computer class:

> I just didn't pay attention in his class because it was all about Microsoft and Power Points and stuff and like I already know stuff about that. It is boring. Well he does this uh, he passes out notes for us to write it down on what we we've already read. I just feel like we, we are writing it for no reason because we've already, like all, I have already learned it, so … I, I don't feel like I need to write notes but he gives us projects like on the computer we have to do and I do those and um … like some other PowerPoint stuff.

Alex's comments show what most students experience in class when teachers do not realize that teaching students requires more than lecturing and note taking. It means encouraging students to make use of their prior knowledge and lived experiences as foundations to promote new learning while becoming critical thinking and life-long learners. Unfortunately, Alex never told his teacher he already knew this lesson or that he was tired of taking notes from slides and Mr. Moose never realized that his lessons were boring and less challenging for Alex. Instead, Mr. Moose interpreted Alex's conformity and invisibility as a good student's expected behavior.

Like Pedro's and Alex's stories of low expectations and feeling disengaged, Julio's Honors U.S. History class observation exemplifies how many Latino boys' experiences are culturally irrelevant and the teacher-centered class encourages them to experience disengagement. Unfortunately, Julio's teacher interpreted his conformity and invisibility as good behavior and his excellent note-taking as good teaching-learning strategies. In my observation notes of Julio's class one day, I wrote:

> The teacher is talking about the Great Depression. He's giving out handouts to students and asking them what caused the Great Depression.
>
> The teacher is lecturing and Julio is listening and taking notes attentively.
>
> The class continues, the teacher keeps lecturing, the students continue taking notes on their handouts. The teacher is the expert; students are empty vessels ready to be filled with knowledge.
>
> The teacher lectures and students take notes from the slides. He asks students some questions but he answers them before the students try to answer them. Julio keeps taking notes quietly. He rubs his eyes again and yawns. Then he stretches.
>
> The teacher is about to give a new set of handouts to students. Students automatically write their names down on their papers. Students are asked to fill out the handouts at home or do it while they watch a video documentary. The class is dark but students need to work on their handouts while they watch the video. Julio starts filling out the handouts. The video starts running, the teacher sits at his desk and starts checking his e-mails. Some students put their heads down while some others work on their assignments.

After my observation of Julio's class, I interviewed Julio and asked what he thought about his class. His response paralleled Alex's and Pedro's stories; he said:

> It was all right. It was kinda of boring. All he does is talk. I mean sometimes it's boring. He doesn't let you fall asleep because he's loud and makes some stuff [the teacher hits a wooden stick against a filing cabinet so students can be awake]. But he's the same the whole time. He's the only one talking. You just listen and take notes.

Even though these boys agreed that taking less challenging courses led them to experience disengagement, they chose to become invisible and to conform to their teachers' expectations in the classroom in order to continue with their studies.

However, when I asked some teachers about Latino boys' motivation in their classrooms, I noticed how their comments focused on what the boys lacked rather than what they contributed. Mr. Sanchez expressed his opinion that girls liked school more than boys. He said:

> For some reason girls ... seem to like school more ... they seem to be more engaged ... more ready academically ... it's almost as if boys ... just do it because they have to ... and girls seem to be more willing to ... to do activities, to learn ... I don't know if it has to do with hormones or what ... but boys are more active, I guess, physically active and the girls are not as active as the boys and so they tend to prefer activities where they don't have to move much.

While Mr. Sanchez referred to "girls seem to like school more" I argue that Latina girls' behavior in the classroom is more connected to issues of conformity and invisibility. Culturally speaking, Latina girls are expected to be docile and obedient toward adult or older masculine figures. Similarly, Mr. Rivers shared:

> I found the that there are many Latino young men that are very hard-working and do what I ask them and are very respectful and feel like they have to work for what they are getting, and I also have some Latino young men that are basically falling into the trap of "society owes me."

Although Mr. Rivers acknowledges that some Latino boys work hard, are respectful, and follow orders (conformity and hidden curriculum), he also perpetuates this idea of blaming the victim when he argues that students "fall into the trap of society owes me" as a form of deficit-model thinking, one which is commonly used to analyze Communities of Color. In a teacher-centered classroom, where lecturing and/or culturally irrelevant lessons take place, some minority students develop anxiety and resistance. A teacher-centered classroom leads students to be disruptive and/or disengaged. The following is my observation of Luis in Mr. Rivers's Algebra class.

> Mr. Rivers looks at me and says to the class, "You'd better hurry up, there's a lesson to teach." Two Latino boys keep talking in the back about something different. Now, the teacher is asking a probability question game. The students who are playing are the only ones paying attention, the rest are having side conversations. The teacher calls students' attention and reminds them that it's educational. One girl is using her cellphone in class; two Latino boys in the back of the classroom keep talking. There

is a Latina girl seated by herself in the back of the room. Something happens and the teacher tries to be funny to the students; some of them start laughing. This class is not engaging anymore.

A white boy puts his head down now and the two Latino boys keep talking. The teacher keeps playing the game with a few white boys and Luis in the front. Another Latino boy in the front is using his cellphone. Luis is very engaged and excited about the game. The students in the back are not engaged at all. I wonder if the teacher prepared his lesson based on his students' learning skills or he just improvised this game this morning. Luis is engaged since he's rolling the dice. The game is over. The teacher gets loud and says, "It took forever." I never saw how this game related to probability since students were not able to discuss probability that much and most of them were not engaged at all.

Mr. Rivers changes the topic and shows a slide of Markov Chains. Luis says he had a friend called Marvok. He encourages the students to take notes. A white student asks Mr. Rivers why he used Markov Chains on the slide. He replies he did it because he couldn't find any other name. Then Mr. Rivers continues explaining the slides and the students keep taking notes. Luis covers his head with a hoody.

The teacher explains a problem and the same few students in the front rows of the class answer his questions. He keeps telling students to take notes from the board. One girl in the front is texting and the teacher asks her to quit it.

Luis pays attention in class. Mr. Rivers tries to be funny when he tells the class that he learned this lesson in fifth grade. He tells the purpose of the lesson was to bore them with games and numbers. He's trying to be on the students' side. But he continues with a new slide. Nine out of 20 students look disengaged in this class.

The teacher keeps talking about probability. He talks and students take notes. Then he stops and tells students they look bored. He continues with his lesson.

Luis is quiet now. He looks bored. Mr. Rivers continues with another slide, some students whine. He tells the class they have 50 seconds to take a nap. The class looks bored at this point. Some students put their heads down. I think the teacher has lost his students' attention. They look tired and disconnected. Luis is silent now. It looked like he was engaged with the game, but now he's not.

While observing Luis in Mr. Rivers's classroom, I noticed how he lost focus, daydreamed, and finally fell asleep. In Luis's Algebra class, Mr. Rivers was teaching about probability in a way that at first actively engaged students using a game on the white board. In my observation, I noticed that only boys expressed enthusiasm about the lesson. Luis was especially engaged because his participation in the game was to roll the dice. However, when the game was over and Mr. Rivers started lecturing, Luis fell asleep for the remainder of the class. Mr. Rivers did not know who I was observing at that time. It was almost the end of the class when I asked Mr. Rivers if I could talk to Luis. When I asked Luis why he was sleeping in class, he told me he had worked until midnight at the pizzeria, so he felt very tired.

Freire (1998) argued that teachers use their "dominant ideology" to blame the students for their own situation (p. 78). Although Mr. Sanchez and Mr. Rivers seem to have high expectations for all students, they agreed that those Latinos who followed the rules succeeded more than those who did not. Interestingly, none of them questioned how their teaching practices might influence student engagement. Both teachers agreed that Latino boys were victims of their own choices, "boys just do it [schoolwork] because they have to" and "society owes me." Both teachers dismissed the possibility that their teaching could be improved and neither took into consideration the wider context of their students' lives or the school's dominant system. Even though they both had the best intentions to teach their lessons, their methods were culturally irrelevant to Latinos/Latinas. Mr. Sanchez's British-version film and Mr. Rivers's lecture about probability pushed most Latino/Latina students to experience disengagement toward real education, not to connect experience with education. The fact that it was a teacher-centered lesson where students could not connect probability to their cultural backgrounds or prior knowledge made it disengaging and irrelevant to all students. Valenzuela (1999) argues that when schools subtract students' cultural, linguistic, and community-based knowledge, students "perceive it as uninteresting, irrelevant, and test-driven" (p. 62). For example, here is my observation of Emilio's Honors Biology class:

> Emilio is quietly copying the information from the board. The lesson is on chromosomes. A student asks a question about the unit, the teacher tells her that he doesn't know the answer. The student encourages the teacher to find the answer. Emilio is quiet. He looks bored now. He puts his hand on his left cheek. He yawns now. The teacher explains the lesson on chromosomes. He reminds students that it is confusing sometimes.

> Emilio has not said a word since I walked into the classroom. He has become invisible the whole time I have been in here. The teacher keeps lecturing the lesson while the students keep taking notes.

I argue that high school students, especially Latinos/Latinas, do not succeed academically, not because they do not take their education as a priority, but because what they understand as education gets reduced to a "banking method" (Freire, 1998) that denies their cultures and their life experiences. I claim that motivating minority students to be engaged and active goes beyond whether girls are more focused on their education than boys and/or following classroom rules. Instead, I posit that motivation takes place when teachers take full responsibility for delivering instruction that is culturally relevant to the students' backgrounds and prior knowledge, and connecting this to what they will need in the future to be successful. Garcia (2001) posits, "Hispanic students at the high school level must be provided with a challenging and integrated curriculum to optimize the opportunities to succeed in life" (p. 189). I add that teachers, especially those who are not socially and culturally related to their students, need to invest some time and get to know their students, their lives, and aspirations beyond the classrooms. Once teachers are able to understand students on a personal level, they both develop a sense of mutual trust and caring. It will lead students to feel *respeto* (respect) for their teachers and what they teach while teachers develop empathy, acceptance, and understanding toward their students.

Conclusion

Like Manny's obstacles in A *Parrot in the Oven*, these boys' counterstories reveal some of the most common barriers Latino teenage boys have to learn to overcome in order to obtain an education. These boys' narratives on gang affiliation, a father's absence, young parenting, low self-esteem, and immigration status shaped their education and personal lives. I posit that it is very important that teachers, school authorities, and parents understand how these social and psychological issues affect Latino boys' lives and education. Alex's and Luis's stories with gangs and parenting show how some Latino teenage boys utilize their cultural capitals as a foundation to develop resiliency and a network orientation. Both boys were outcasts in school as troublemakers and both decided to challenge these negative assumptions and stayed in school. Juan's and Jose's status as undocumented immigrants also challenge what most studies say about Latino students dropping out of school due to their immigration status. Both of these young boys used their familial and aspirational capitals to resist oppression and people's expectations based on their legal status. In addition, both developed their own social and navigational capitals as part of their network orientation (Stanton-Salazar & Spina, 2000) that allowed them to cross socio-cultural borders. They claim:

> A network orientation reflects a consciousness which facilitates the crossing of socio-cultural borders, the overcoming of institutional barriers, and the individual's active participation in multiple kinship, community, and institutional settings where supportive relations can be cultivated and exercised. (p. 247)

They add, "An individual's network orientation can be seen through multiple forms of knowledge, perceptions, attitudes, beliefs, dispositions, and social competencies" (Stanton-Salazar & Spina, 2000, p. 247). Through examining these boy's stories through a community cultural wealth lens, we can see that the development of a network orientation to remain in school represents the next phase after becoming resilient.

In their own communities Latino boys are entitled to experience more freedom than girls. However, that freedom encourages them to become more vulnerable to legal trouble, leading them to develop a hypermasculinity. I argue that allowing boys to experience a street culture too often leads them to get in trouble for breaking the law and to become more vulnerable to other social problems such as drugs, alcohol, teenage pregnancy, and unplanned parenthood.

Although none of these boys' counterstories showed them as examples of being tough, rude, angry, and violent to authority figures, in my years of teaching, I witnessed how other Latino boys became targets for racial profiling and negative assumptions about them as gang members, drug dealers, idlers, or troublemakers. Unfortunately, most of those boys had no choice other than dropping out of school. Most of them end up working in low-wage jobs, starting their own families, getting in jail for breaking the law, being deported back to their countries, or getting killed.

Valenzuela (1999) claims that immigrant and U.S.-born youth are entitled to receive "an authentic form of caring that emphasizes relations of reciprocity between teachers and students" (p. 61). Although teachers recognized Latino boys as hard workers, they also claimed that it is the boys' personal decision to do wrong in school (meritocracy) and/or lack of assimilation (deficit-thinking model). Tatum (2007) argues, "teachers need to learn about the students' lives, their cultural, socioeconomic, and sociopolitical contexts before making assumptions about their identities" (p. 27). I argue that teachers and school administrators need to develop a reciprocal relationship with Latino boys where they can be seen as positive role models and caring human beings. In the last chapter, I also discuss how teachers and school administrators are caught in a structural system that promotes inequity and inequality in Communities of Color.

In *A Parrot in the Oven*, Manny realizes that to be in a gang is not the best choice for him. He learns that as "*perico*" he lives in an oven called society, so he has to be smart enough so negative influences cannot burn him. These boys' counterstories show how living in an "oven" makes boys of color, in this case Latino boys, experience vulnerability at school and in their communities. Some boys show frustration and anger because they do not know how to handle life and family obstacles, using the school as an outlet to release their problems or to forget about them. However, those messages are sometimes misunderstood as resistance and disruptive behavior, leading these boys to become targeted and punished by teachers and school authorities. Like Manny and these boys, some boys learn how to use their cultural capitals to develop resiliency and a network support that allows them to remain in school and do well in life. I argue that schools do not represent nurturing spaces with a culturally relevant curriculum where students of color feel welcomed and empowered. Instead, students of color are treated as deficient. Boys of color are still seen as a threat to the community and the school. As a result, some of these boys develop a hypermasculinity of resistance to challenge an intolerant society and white school culture that pushes them to become more and more vulnerable to punishment, incarceration, and death. The next chapter will unearth how some motivational factors allow these Latino boys to remain in school. I will also unveil how these boys' expectations about themselves challenge what their teachers believe about Latino teenage boys.

· 3 ·

EL QUE PERSEVERA TRIUNFA
(WHOEVER PERSEVERES, TRIUMPHS)

When I started teaching high school in North Carolina in 1999, it was very difficult for some Latino/Latina teenagers to remain in school. A few of them had already quit their schools back home before even entering the U.S., and some others never completed elementary or middle school. Others did not know how to deal with issues of discrimination, the new language at school, and new cultural ways of being in U.S. society. Most of them, especially boys, decided to quit school to support their parents, help their younger siblings, and/or send money back home. There were only a few boys who decided to challenge society and expectations of failure and remain in school.

There were times when I felt frustrated and overwhelmed from witnessing so many Latino students abandon school to join their parents and friends in factories, landscaping, and/or fast food restaurants. Since some became young parents and felt the responsibility of their new roles as parents, their education was no longer a priority. Some thought that because of their immigration status in the country, it was a waste of time to be in school if they could not attend college. Others got in trouble with the law and ended up in jail or dead.

In the 2011–2012 school year, I co-taught an English III course. Most of the students in this regular course were students of color; most of them were

Latino boys. My main role was to support my English as a Second Language (ESL) students. I already knew some of these students since some were English language learners (ELLs) and the rest met me in this class. My co-teacher and I struggled to maintain discipline and students' attendance was low.

In this English course, I learned that Luis and Felipe (pseudonyms) were already parents. I also learned that both teenage boys had part-time jobs, and experienced problems with their girlfriends and school. Both of them sometimes missed school when their children were sick or when they had to take them to the doctor. In the middle of the semester, Felipe dropped out of school because his girlfriend did not get along with his parents, so he needed to get a full-time job to support his child and to find a place to live with his new family. Even though I tried to convince Felipe to stay in school, he felt he had no choice but to drop out of school.

During that time I developed a close teacher-student relationship with Luis. I tried to help him on his senior project. This sense of caring allowed me to gain his *confianza* (trust). Stanton-Salazar (2001) claims, "*Confianza* allows people to engage in important transactions without fear of being deliberately deceived and used" (p. 27). During this process, I always wondered what kept Luis in school. It was the norm that most Latino/Latina students who became parents or had constant discipline problems dropped out of school. I always wanted to find out what structure or system outside the school supported Luis and the other boys to stay in school.

In order to voice the experiences of some Latino boys who decide to challenge school norms, like Luis and his peers, this chapter illustrates the counterstories of nine Latino boys and the motivational factors that encouraged them to remain in school. These boys' counterstories show how through self-motivation, parental influence and lived experiences, fatherhood, support of friends, sports, and the expression *échale ganas* (do your best) as a form of resiliency, the students were able to develop a network orientation that allowed them to focus on their education. I argue that when school systems lump Latino boys as uninterested and resistant to being too Americanized as a synonym of for laziness or "society owes me," their comments perpetuate a deficit-thinking model theory. A deficit-thinking model suggests that when a student fails in school, it is because he or she has internal deficits or deficiencies associated with "intellectual abilities, linguistic shortcomings, lack of motivation to learn, and immoral behavior" (Valencia, 2010, p. 7). In spite of the fact that the majoritarian assumptions and culturally biased studies analyze Latino boys' failure in school as normal (Valencia, 2010), in my study,

I analyze how these nine Latino boys' counternarratives unveil how their hard work and goals toward a high school education and beyond are connected to their community cultural wealth (Yosso, 2006b), resiliency, and a network orientation (Stanton-Salazar & Spina, 2000). I found in these boys' counternarratives two common threads: (a) their abilities to maintain high goals in the face of adversity, and (b) the importance of a kinship unit and a support network that motivated them to stay in school.

Motivational Factors to Remain in School

Stanton-Salazar and Spina (2000) claim that resiliency is a developmental process in which "psychological attributes and defenses lay the groundwork for later network dispositions, relational patterns, social competencies, and experiences" (p. 245). In order to unpack why these boys decided to remain in school, I unearth how these boys' counternarratives unveil the development of resiliency and a network structure that allowed them to navigate the educational system. This resiliency develops from their own expectations, their parents' influence and lived experiences, as well as their own experiences as parents, friends' support, and *échale ganas* (do your best).

Self-Motivated

Early in my study during the first conversations, I asked these boys, "Do you believe that the fact that you look Latino affects how you do in school?" Most of them stated that race has nothing to do with academic performance. Instead, they agreed that it was a personal choice since some Latino boys pushed themselves to get good grades. Luis said, "It depends on the person because there are other kids that … They're the same as me but they do better. I guess they push themselves some more … it might just depend on the individual himself." Emilio agreed, "Not really, I think if I do as any other race, I think that factor affects my grade, my education." He shared that he had never been treated differently just because he was a Latino boy, since he liked to study, "I try to put my best effort." Alex suggested that anybody can do well in school, "You have to put your best effort into it and try." Similarly, Julio agreed that race does not determine academic failure or success. He said,

No, it has nothing to do with it. I mean. I guess your race has anything to do with what you do in school. Is completely different … let's see, it doesn't have anything to do with because race is something you are and school is something you have to do, so it doesn't really mix. It doesn't have anything to do with it.

Julio expressed that he had never been treated differently for being Latino and that race did not determine one's academic success. He, like the other boys, agreed that success in school was more a personal choice.

Although these boys agreed that it depends on how motivated the individual feels about his/her education and that race and gender had nothing to do with it, in the next chapter of this book, these Latino boys' counterstories unpack how their experiences with different layers of discrimination as Latino boys influenced their education and well-being.

Parents' Influence and Lived Experiences

Most of the participants shared how their parents' influence and lived experiences pushed them to remain in school. For example, Carlos's mother decided to move to the Southeast to avoid any problems that could affect Carlos's education. He shared that students in his previous school showed a lot of behavioral problems, so he preferred to stay home. Carlos also explained that before moving to this school, his mother sent him to live with his dad due to his lack of motivation for schooling. He shared:

> My mom used to get really mad; she made me move with my father 'cause she knows I listen to my father more, so I had to live with him … he straightened me up. So I started doing better in school, paying attention more.

During the conversations, Carlos shared that his father had a lot of influence on him. Even though they did not see each other on a regular basis, Carlos's father phoned him and cared about his education and well-being. Since Carlos's goal was to become a business owner like his father, I asked him what motivated him to come to school. He said:

> My father, I look up to him; he's my role model in my life. He always wants me to be in school, he wants me to have a good future because he always tells me that he had a rough childhood. He works seven days a week in his restaurant, so he wants me to not work as hard as he does … to have a more successful life.

Carlos's parents emphasized to him that his only way to succeed in life was through education. Although Carlos's father was not physically present, his regular communication with Carlos affected his life positively. Often parents use their own personal experiences as part of their familial and aspirational capital to teach their children about life, what to do, and what to avoid. Carlos's counternarrative explained what many Latino/Latina students endure. Even though he was not making the highest grades, he was resilient and stayed in school; his parents, especially his father, helped and motivated him. His parents' advice and family goals instilled in him encouraged him to remain in school. Also, being the oldest child and the only "man" in the house placed him in a position of responsibility and commitment. He became the protector, and a male figure for his little sister. During our second conversation, I asked the boys how their parents and other relatives' life experiences influenced their life and education.

Raúl: My parents didn't have the best education at the time, so they always encourage me to do good at school, you know ... to have a better future.

Emilio: They make me not take things for granted and to do better and to do my best in school so I can have a better life than they do.

Julio: They like tell you about the experiences they had done like not to make the same mistakes. They tell you to pick something good and follow with it.

José: They tell me like to learn from other people's mistakes and to do better than them.

Carlos: My father always tells me to do good in school because he never went to high school and he doesn't have a degree and he always tells me how hard he has to work every single day in his business. He doesn't want me to make the same mistakes as his. He wants me to have a better life than he has.

Pedro: My parents always encourage me to pursue education because education is important like now why do hard work when you are old like useless when you can do the hard work now and that will pay off in the long run. Why work in a factory when you can become a doctor working barely long hours and making big cash.

All of these boys agreed that since most of their parents came to this country due to financial problems and to look for a better future, the best way to overcome poverty and to be successful was usually related to getting an education to help their *familias*. Stanton-Salazar and Spina (2000) posit that resiliency in youth minority develops when trust within family and the community exists as a form of support to overcome negative forces around them: "Cultural ideologies, and ethnic support systems promulgate expectations for ongoing exchange, mutual generosity, and reciprocity in the context of trusting" (p. 246).

Most of these boys agreed that their parents immigrated to the United States looking for a better future so the only way to pay them back or to make them feel proud was through their education. Emilio said:

> What motivates me is my mom; my mom has had very hard troubles since she doesn't have the required education to get most jobs. She started up cleaning toilets in a bank; she had no money, no food, no shelter or anything. She basically had nothing; she lived on the side of a house that a friend of a friend that she knew. She basically built up from that. She's always telling me to continue learning. Don't ever take things for granted because she never had the opportunities that I have now that can help me succeed in life more than what she had. She wants me to be bigger than what she was, to have more things than what she did.

Emilio internalized his parents' hardships before and while living in the United States.

Like Emilio's parents, most immigrant families have to start their new lives by doing tough jobs, relying on their children who can later teach them how to navigate the American system. Most of the boys agreed that their parents were their biggest motivation to be in school. Alex, who experienced being targeted as a gang member and recruiter by some teachers, said: "My mom is always telling [me] to try to do good in school … I'm trying to make them [parents] proud, not make it a waste that they just came over here for nothing." Even though Alex shared that he used to be a "Latin King" (the name of a gang), he still wanted to succeed in life.

José's motivation came from his aspirations to become a professional soccer player to support his mother and make his family feel proud of him. Julio also agreed that his motivation came from his parents: "I guess my parents motivate me to go to college, get an education so you don't have to suffer in life about economic problems. You could have economic opportunities in the future where you don't have to work very hard like they did."

I found that these boys' counterstories about motivation were embedded in their community cultural wealth, which helped them to be resilient. Salazar-Stanton and Spina (2000) posit that resiliency as a developmental path allows individuals to make use of their available resources and assets to cope with "adversities and environmental stressors" (p. 245). All boys shared how their parents constantly reminded them how hard their lives were before coming to this country while using their current lifestyle as life examples for their own children. These constant reminders develop in immigrants a sense of moral obligation to do well in school and in life in order to give back to their parents and to become role models for their siblings or closest relatives. Cammarota

(2008) claims that in Latino families the older generation is expected to give back to a new generation as a way to thank them for what they got when they were younger. The participants used their familial and aspirational capitals when talking about their parents', relatives', and friends' common knowledge, as well as their own aspirations to complete high school and to continue their studies.

Fatherhood

Gándara and Contreras (2009) posit that research studies found that half of Latino teenagers have experienced sexual intercourse by the time they reach 17 years of age. They suggest that the perception that Latino adolescents' peers are involved in sexual behavior can lead other Latino teenagers to imitate similar patterns. When I co-taught an English class at the high school, I knew I wanted Luis to be part of my book. I really came to admire Luis's determination to be in school after becoming a father at a young age. I always considered him an exception to the rule since most young parents like him end up dropping out. Luis's parents split up by the time he knew he was becoming a father, so he decided to live with his father while the rest of his siblings moved in with his mother. In the following conversation, Luis shared how his relationship with his father motivated him to attend school.

R.V.:	Who or what motivates you to come to school?
Luis:	Well, it's my dad first, my dad and my son.
R.V.:	Talk to me about your dad and then your son.
Luis:	My dad because he gives me what I want, he tries to give me the best what I need and stuff, so that's why I wanna do it for him.
R.V.:	Are you very close to your dad?
Luis:	Yeah.
R.V.:	You said my son, talk to me about that.
Luis:	Well, I don't want him to go like "my dad is fine without a high school diploma so I can too."
R.V.:	So you want to be a role model for your child?
Luis:	Yes.

Luis was a senior and his academic performance and school behavior were not that good. He missed many days after he was accused of bullying a white boy. His absences and long working hours at the pizza restaurant affected his school. Most of his grades were C's and D's; the only A's were in Physical Education and Foods. Those classes were ones where physical skill and ability were needed as much as academic recall and were classes that his peers regarded as safe and easy. Although his grades were not high, in the context of the larger responsibilities he had, he was striving to stay in school doing the best he could, given his circumstances. Fatherhood both made this difficult and motivated him. It is important to note that the norm is for most Latino boys to drop out of school and find a job to cope with their new responsibilities of being a father. Contrary to this normalcy, Luis's parents, especially his father, encouraged him to stay in school and get a high school diploma. Although in this book Luis was the one participant who became a father while still in high school, his counterstory represented an anomaly. Most Latino boys who become parents are expected to cope with their new roles' responsibilities of getting a job to support their new families. This new role and responsibility oblige most of them to drop out of school. Further in this chapter, I unearth how Luis struggled while attending school full-time and working part-time in a fast food restaurant.

Network Orientation: Friends and Sports

In my years of teaching, I witnessed how many Latino/Latina students developed a network where they encouraged one another to learn how to cope with school and family issues. In this section, I discuss how these boys found strong supportive networks through their friends, local institutions, and sports, which allowed them to remain in school. Stanton-Salazar and Spina (2000) posit that the development of a positive "help-seeking orientation" is fundamental to resiliency during adolescence. They claim:

> A truly cosmopolitan network orientation reflects a consciousness, which facilitates the crossing of sociocultural borders, the overcoming of institutional barriers, and the individuals' active participation in multiple kinship, community, and institutional settings where supportive relations can be cultivated and exercised. (pp. 246–247)

During the conversations, Juan mentioned that he was not living with parents and siblings but with two friends, whom I happened to know as members of the local community. Rosa (pseudonym) was a Latina woman from California, and Sarah (pseudonym) was a local white woman. Juan met Rosa when he was still in middle school and used to spend most of his afternoons at the public library where Rosa worked part-time. Both Rosa and Sarah developed a close relationship with Juan, like that of mother and child. Later, after some arguments with his oldest brother, Juan moved into Rosa's and Sarah's house. Even though Juan still visited his parents, he did not feel any connections with them in terms of motivation and school success. His biggest inspiration to be in school came from Rosa and Sarah. When I asked him about what motivated him to stay in school, he said:

> Rosa ... because when I lived with my parents I was good in school, but they never checked my work, they never said good job, this and that. And her, if I needed to do better, she [Rosa] was like you need to do better because it's not acceptable, this and that. And it made me feel good because someone was paying attention to me and were not my parents. Sarah does it too, like I got a C in my report card in personal finance and she was like your report card is good except that C. Let's work on it and get straight A's next time. And that makes me feel good because there is somebody who is paying attention to me, and they care about my grades and everything.

Having adults who cared about his work and his grades mattered. Contrary to what dominant assumptions and societal structures think about teenage boys as resistant and uninterested in their education, boys like Juan need to feel that somebody cares about them and their education. They need to understand that someone is there for them to support and to encourage them to do better in life and to remain in school. While writing this book, I learned that Rosa had moved back to California, so Juan was living with Sarah and her little boy. Rosa kept in touch with Juan. She called him and advised him about school and life. Juan was still doing well in school, but he shared that sometimes he missed his mother. He said that he visited her sometimes but did not want to move back home with his parents, "I miss them but ... I don't wanna go back to how it was before ... I like how I am now ... changed, a new person, I can say." Nonetheless, Juan still missed his mother, "like sometimes the food ... like sometimes my mom ... she used to hug me ... like for my birthday or Mother's Day, she gave a hug ... little stuff like that." During our conversations, Juan never expressed positive words about his father. Instead, he criticized him for letting his oldest brother play the father role, which was the main reason Juan left the house.

Similar to Juan's counterstories on developing a network orientation (Stanton-Salazar & Spina, 2000) as part of resiliency to remain in school, some other boys shared how, through sports, they developed their own social and navigational capitals. Most of them expressed how playing sports not only allowed them to focus on their education but to forget about their family problems or to avoid getting involved in gang-related activities. Pedro shared:

I started doing football and wrestling when I was in seventh grade. I guess I started doing sports when I was in seventh and then I didn't do eighth grade. I always wanted to do wrestling; that's probably the main sport, like that's pretty much what I am all about. I love wrestling. I still keep on doing it.

Like Pedro, most of these boys enjoyed playing soccer, football, and basketball. José, Luis, and Alex played on the school soccer team, becoming outstanding players. Likewise, Emilio and Julio belonged to the school track team. Stanton-Salazar and Spina (2000) argue:

Successful and simultaneous participation across disparate and conflictive social worlds becomes synonymous with the development of an interpersonal (egocentric) network with structural features which reveal numerous social ties across both overlapping and unlocking social networks. (p. 242)

Most of these boys found the resources to develop their social and navigational capitals that led them to experience acceptance at school and in the community. Juan's counterstories showed how through his friend he gained access to a local institution where he found people who cared and supported his personal life and education. Likewise, most of the boys agreed that when they play sports, other people do not see them as Latino boys anymore, but as good athletes. These boys, because of their resiliency and the development of a network orientation, were able to cross social and racial borders in order to join sports and to navigate local institutions.

Échale Ganas as Resiliency

To develop their potential for healthy social development, low-income minority youth need to receive emotional and social resources usually found within the family unit. In this section, I unpack how *échale ganas* (do your best), as a cultural asset, is used among these boys and their families to develop resilience to remain in school in spite of their personal and/or family problems.

During the first conversation, I asked these boys to define the expression *échale ganas*. I explained to them that this expression was very common in Mexico and that some other Latin American countries used a similar expression. Most of the participants agreed that *échale ganas* meant to work hard in order to pursue success. Juan commented, "striving for success to pursue your dreams and get a career." Emilio added, "to try your best to keep forward and don't let anybody stop you." Pedro and José agreed that *échale ganas* meant that hard work and dedication would pay off. After this session, I mentioned to these boys that I was using *échale ganas* as an important phrase in my study. Even though I did not bring up this phrase anymore during our gatherings, some of the participants mentioned it frequently during our conversations, referring to it as a form of resiliency to keep trying hard while remaining in school.

While interviewing José, I asked him what worried him the most. He shared that although he always worried about his future, he kept trying hard. José said:

> My studies thing ... like there are some guys born here y *no le échan ganas* (don't do their best) ... and then ... I don't wanna be like them. *Que na' más queman su record and este así como los Mexicans que nacen en Mexico y le echan ganas.* (They ruin their record and like Mexicans who are born in Mexico and do their best.) Yeah. *Porque (los Mexicanos) llegaron aquí por una razón, por problemas económicos pa' echarle ganas. Esa es una de las razones que ... te ayudan* (because they [Mexicans] came here for a reason for financial problems to do their best. That is a way that they help to) succeed in life. *Porque aquí, si yo nací aquí y yo quemo mi record por pelearme a mí no me echan pa' mi país porque yo nací aquí.* (Because here, if I were born here and I ruin my record for fighting, they don't deport me back to my country because I was born here).

José explained that some U.S.-born Latino/Latina students take for granted the fact that they were born here, so they are not afraid to be deported if they do something bad. He argued that undocumented Mexican students work hard since they came here due to their families' financial problems. José voiced a complaint often made by undocumented students who want to continue their education; this is a generalization that undocumented Mexican students work hard. However, in this case I felt his comments were very personal and insightful. Valenzuela (1999) suggests "immigrant groups differ from U.S. born youth in their tendency to combine *empeño* with other resources in a collectivistic fashion" (p. 141). I add that Valenzuela's *empeño*, which she translates as diligence is closely related to *échale ganas a la escuela* (do your best in school.) However, Váldes (1996) recommends that we should not make generalizations about the Mexican origin population with regard to their education success or failure since most of them possess generational, regional, experiential, and linguistic differences. Even though José was aware of his immigration status and how challenging it would be for him to pursue higher education in this country, he still used his familial and aspirational capitals to stay in school and try hard to achieve his goal of getting a high school diploma, going to college, and becoming a professional soccer player.

Like José, Luis's comments showed how his father's words of encouragement pushed him to develop resiliency toward his education. He said, "See my dad works in a furniture factory. Tells me *Que le eche ganas* (to do my best) so I don't have to be working *como un burro, como él* (like a donkey, like him). So I guess that is like pushing me." His father's lived experiences made Luis realize that if he focused on his education, he would not end up working in a factory, making a minimum salary. Similarly, Juan's resiliency came from his friends at the local library who encouraged and supported his education. He shared:

> Like when they saw my report card and they saw a B and like I know you can do better. Like we believe in you and they took me to do stuff. Like Ms. Daisy [pseudonym] before she died, she took me to eat and bought me clothes. She bought me a tux for the Beta Club, initiation in seventh grade and just that little stuff helps, made me believe in myself.

Even though Juan's parents did not provide direct words of encouragement toward his education, he used his social and navigational capitals to find a support network at the local library. Similarly, Emilio shared how his mother supported his education and academic success. He stated:

> She's always telling me to continue learning. Don't ever take things for granted because she never had the opportunities that I have now that can help me succeed in life more than what she wants. She wants me to be bigger than what she was, to have more things than what she did.

Because of his close relationship with his mother, Emilio, like many other Latino/Latina students, used his parents' lived experiences to *echarle ganas* and to develop resiliency. Such students learn how to use their own social and navigational capitals in their communities, so it is easy for them to develop the necessary networks to support their parents, relatives, and friends.

Carlos's *échale ganas* counterstory referred to having courage to do his best in life. He mentioned that even though he messed up with his grades, he still developed some type of courage to keep on trying. He said, "I still have to do it and get over the obstacle and keep doing." He commented that he wanted to see himself succeed in life and become a role model for younger generations regardless of those obstacles. He said, "I wanna tell somebody when I am older, Yeah, I've been through that, I've done that. I've gone through those obstacles, and I still succeeded."

Most of these boys unveiled how *échale ganas* became a motivational factor while remaining in school. They learned to develop their own strategies to overcome life obstacles and to encounter hope. They developed their navigational and social capitals to identify ways to pursue higher education in the U.S. Most of the other boys used sports as a vehicle to build resiliency and a supportive network orientation.

Conclusion

Even if few in number, there are students who manage to maintain their identities and achieve academically without being ostracized by their peers. Understanding how such students navigate this difficult terrain may be the key to figuring out how to support the achievement of larger numbers of Black [and Latino/Latina] students. (Noguera, 2008, p. 32)

Like Noguera and many other scholars who inspired me to write my book, I believe it is important to continue exploring what forces help Latino boys to remain in school to challenge social norms and a deficit-thinking model. These boys' cultural capital represented the main resource for them to remain in school. Some of them shared that even though they were not excellent students, they still kept coming to school in order to pay their parents back for their life sacrifices. Even though some of them were born and raised in this country, it was evident that their parents' stories before, during, and after they immigrated to this country were internalized by most of these boys. Their parents' stories became part of the community cultural wealth that kept them in school. Most of them talked about how much their parents suffered in poverty and lack of opportunities in their countries. They shared how their parents let them know about the opportunities they could have if they remained in school. Some parents even used their current jobs to teach these boys about their futures if they did not study hard. Like Emilio, some of these boys shared how seeing their parents' hard work motivated them to focus on their studies. In addition, the use of their parents' linguistic capital with the expression *échale ganas* (do your best), which is part of the title in my book represents a form of resiliency to keep working hard and never give up. Through these counterstories, I heard these boys found encouragement from their parents. Even though some of them were experiencing family and personal problems, they developed their own agency to navigate and to resist school and social obstacles. For example, Juan developed his own agency through his friends Rosa and Sarah, who helped him to navigate a local institution where he felt cared for and appreciated.

These nine boys represent a small number of those Latino/Latina students who persevere in school through hard work. Contrary to traditional studies that understand cultures of students of color as obstacles to succeed academically (Valencia, 2010), I claim that teachers, school administrators, and stakeholders need to build upon the cultural wealth of Communities of Color to foster and motivate them to stay in school. Garcia (2001) argues, "The challenge facing educators with regard to Hispanic students is not to 'Americanize' them. Instead, it is to understand them and act responsibly to the specific diversity that they bring and the educational goal of academic success for all students" (p. 51). School systems need to see minority students as cultural assets that can enrich not only the school but also their communities. Students of color internalize that they and their cultural backgrounds are not appreciated in the schools. Instead, they understand that as a norm to succeed in this country, they need to assimilate to white American dominant culture. Some of them feel disengaged, unmotivated, and resistant to succeed. Some others, like these nine boys, *le echan ganas* (do their best) to learn to develop their own networking support, using their community cultural wealth as a springboard to become resilient and remain in school, following their parents' and friends' *consejo* (advice) *El que persevera, triunfa* (Whoever perseveres, triumphs).

· 4 ·

JUNTOS PERO NO REVUELTOS
(TOGETHER BUT NOT THE SAME)

Although labeling itself is not the cause of students' failure to complete their schooling, it creates a set of expectations and stigmas for those so labeled that can suppress
the drive to achieve academically. (Wise, 2010, p. 105)

In most Latin American countries issues of race and racism are institutionalized as a result of colonialism, imperialism, and capitalism. Unfortunately,
the vast majority of oppressed people, especially indigenous and Black people,
have learned to experience discrimination as normal, leading oppressed Latin
American societies to focus on issues of classism and gender discrimination
more than any other layer of oppression. Latin Americans talk about racism
as a legacy of slavery and colonialism, "Racial inequality is regarded as the
product of class dynamics" (Bonilla-Silva, 2010, p. 181). Even though most
Latin American immigrants to this country are grouped under one umbrella
by making us a single and static group, many of us claim to be different from
each other in many aspects. Many of us refuse to identify ourselves in racial or
Hispanic/Latino terms. However, our immigration histories and experiences
with gender, race, ethnicity, class, phenotype, and location shape our new
identities in this country. Some of us have developed a stronger sense of pride
in our homelands for being immigrants to this country while some others
prefer to attempt to assimilate the dominant culture in hopes of blending in

and accessing upward mobility. *Juntos pero no revueltos* (Together but not the same) encompasses a claim that some of the Latino boys voiced in their counterstories. *Juntos* (together) because they shared the same gender, location, age, ethnicity, language, and community cultural capitals; *pero no revueltos* (but not the same) because their personal counterstories explored how being Latin American immigrants and U.S.-born Latinos with different cultural and socio-economic backgrounds and immigration histories challenge the idea of a homogeneous and static Latino group.

In this chapter I unearth how, using *Latinidades* as a common thread, the participants' struggle to preserve their heritage language is part of their linguistic capital and a form of resistance. I also explore how the use of pan-ethnic labels affects the participants' self-identities and school performance while intersecting other layers of oppression. In addition, I analyze how these students' experiences with punishment at school align with previous research studies. Finally, I discuss how these boys' counter-narratives with *vergüenza* (shame) relate to issues of ethnicity, phenotype, class, and immigration status in this country.

When Labels Hurt

Although *Latinidades* has often been used to analyze a common identity as Latin Americans and U.S. Latinos, some scholars have used it to challenge dominant ideologies of immigration, (post) (neo) colonialism, race, color, legal status, class, nation, and language in the United States (Rodriguez, 2003; Román & Sandoval, 1997). De Genova and Ramos-Zayas (2003) argue that the only commonalities that Latin American countries share are in relation to "the colonial and imperialist projects throughout Latin America, in concert with the concomitant historical as well as contemporary racialization of both Latin America, as a whole, and Latinos in the U.S. in relation to a sociopolitical order of white supremacy" (p. 21). They suggest that Latin Americans and U.S. Latinos/Latinas should develop coalitions across lines of difference instead of the dominant ideology of a single and static Latino culture.

Español

The Latino teenage boys in this book acknowledged the importance of preserving their Spanish language as their linguistic capital and as a form of resiliency. Students of color possess many languages and communication skills as part of their linguistic capitals (Yosso, 2006b). During the first conversation, I asked the boys how important it was for them to keep their Spanish language skills. Alex and Carlos agreed that it was important for them to communicate with their grandparents who were still living back in their Latin American countries. Alex said, "I think is pretty important because when let's say I go back to visit my grandparents to Guatemala, I can't just be like stuttering." Emilio, José, Luis, and Juan claimed that being bilingual allowed them to get better jobs with good salaries since they could communicate and translate in two different languages.

Carlos also commented that preserving his heritage language was very important since his grandparents could not speak English, but he also pointed out how difficult it was for him to speak Spanish since he never learned it at school. He said:

> Is important but is *kinda* of hard because my whole I life I have spoken English. I never really learned Spanish unless it's a Spanish class or I hear my mother talk or when my grandma came to visit. She only speaks Spanish, my grandfather only speaks Spanish. And he lived here for a couple of years so I started to learn more and more Spanish. But speaking it is sometimes difficult 'cause when I have a word in my head I know how to say it in English but it doesn't come right in Spanish. I just keep trying to [speak it].

Like Carlos, Pedro shared that speaking Spanish was hard for him since he found learning English easier even though his parents tried to teach him to speak Spanish when he was little. He stated that he understood when people talked in Spanish but he had difficulties answering back in Spanish, so he'd rather use his English language instead: "I understand what they are saying [his parents] in Spanish, but like responding back in Spanish is a little bit difficult, so I mispronounce some words. But I understand what they are saying, so I talk back to them in English."

When I asked the boys what they did to maintain their heritage language, most of them agreed that they practiced it at home with their parents and siblings; others said they practiced it at school or were taking Spanish courses. However, some of them admitted having difficulties writing and reading it. Carlos shared, "Reading is *kinda* difficult, but writing is worse ... I am not good at writing in Spanish, so I am taking Spanish next semester, Spanish two." Others like Pedro argued that even though he was taking a Spanish course at school, he felt that he was not learning that much, "I feel like I am wasting my time in that class sometimes. Sometimes I feel that is one of the reasons I slack off. I fall asleep because it is too easy. I know most of the stuff they go over."

Like Carlos, many students complained when they were placed in Spanish I or II since they had already mastered most of the curriculum their teachers were addressing in class. Even though Carlos argued that he wanted a more challenging class, he also acknowledged that this class was an easy way for him to get a good grade on his foreign language credits.

Most of these boys agreed that using their Spanish language was a way to communicate with their relatives and to earn more money as a bilingual. Unfortunately, like many schools in the southeastern United States, these boys' school did not have a strong curriculum for Spanish speakers that could have prepared them to be fully bilingual in both languages. Suárez-Orozco and Suárez-Orozco (2001) claim:

> When immigrant children master competencies in two languages they develop "transcultural identities" which become essential part of their sense of self. Having "transcultural identities" allows immigrant children to "easily communicate with members of their own ethnic group as well as with students, teachers, employers, and colleagues of other backgrounds." (p. 113)

These boys' lack of a serious curriculum in Spanish will lead them to be *perdido en dos mundos* (lost in two worlds). Most of them will still be able to understand spoken Spanish but will be limited in their reading and writing skills. It is important to understand that their heritage language often got stuck in the time and space when their parents decided to immigrate to this country. If the school system does nothing to address teaching Spanish to native speakers to increase cultural capital, Latino students will internalize a sense of being *perdido en dos mundos*. They are likely to feel lost in their own communities for not being able to connect with their parents, relatives, and friends in their heritage language, and lost in the dominant group since being Latino/Latina will always make them the *Other*. In the last chapter, I will address how some of these boys, like many other Latino/Latina students in this country, become illiterate in both languages. What happens when *Latinidades*, as a synonym of a common culture, are used to oppress Latino boys in school? In the next section, I analyze how these boys' experiences are impacted by gender and phenotype.

Skin Tone

> For children, the process of becoming American today has itself taken a new turn and may now include the adoption or rejection of such constructed pan-ethnic categories as Hispanic and Asian/Pacific Islander, which lump together scores of nationalities into one-size-fits-all minority group labels. (Portes & Rumbaut, 2001, p. 150)

Since my intention in this book is to challenge the dominant idea of a homogenous Latino culture, during the interviews I purposefully asked Carlos, Emilio, Alex, Raúl, and Julio whose cultural backgrounds were different than most Latino students (because most Latino students in the area are from Mexico) if somebody had ever referred to them as Mexicans because of their skin color, physical appearance, or their Spanish-speaking skills. Carlos, whose parents came to this country from the Dominican Republic, shared this story.

Carlos:	I really know what you are saying, like I don't really like when people call me Mexican just because I am Hispanic. It really offends me when somebody calls me Mexican. The other day in class the teacher said the majority of Hispanics dishes, she said it in general, are made with cheese and meat. I am Dominican; we never eat cheese for dinner, that's more a Mexican tradition to eat cheese and meat.
R.V.:	Did you feel offended?
Carlos:	Yes, *kinda* … in general we are not the same; we are all different.
R.V.:	How do you make that distinction at school?
Carlos:	I just tell them I am not Mexican; I am Dominican. We are both Hispanics, but we are not all the same. The way we [Dominicans] talk is different.

Portes and Rumbaut (2001) argue that adolescents "compare themselves with those around them based on their social similarities—especially with regard to socially visible categorized markers as gender, phenotype, language, and nationality" (p. 151). Emilio and Alex, whose parents came from Cuba and Guatemala, respectively, both shared stories of being called Mexican because of their skin tone and Spanish-speaking skills; however, neither of them ever took it as an insult. Emilio argued that being called Mexican was not the same thing as being called Hispanic, which implied that everybody was the same. Portes and Rumbaut (2001) claim, "ethnic identification begins with the application of a label to oneself in a cognitive process of self-categorization" (p. 151). Alex shared that he only reminded people he was not from Mexico. However, he stated that his answer was different depending on the race/ethnicity of the person asking. He stated, "If it's a white person, I tell him; I am as white as you are; I was born here." Carlos's answer reflected how he resisted oppression from a white person addressing him as "Mexican," the *Other*, because of his skin tone, Mesoamerican (indigenous) appearance, and network of Latino/Latina friends. It is not that he was claiming being white, as a race, because he was born in this country. Instead, he was stating to his white peers that he possessed the same rights as a U.S. citizen. Carlos internalized that because he looked Mexican to them, he was assumed to be in this country illegally and considered less than whites. Although Carlos never enjoyed institutionalized white privilege, he still tried to challenge the norm. In their study, De Genova and Ramos-Zayas (2003) found that depending on context the individual can internalize the label "Mexican" as an "intrinsically derogatory racist slur" (p. 177). According to them, individuals prefer to be referred to as Latinos. In my experience as a teacher, community member, and scholar in this country, I have witnessed how having a different complexion beyond the Black/White binary and speaking English with or without an accent make an individual vulnerable to be labeled Mexican or Asian. I argue that when individuals are stereotyped pan-ethnic labels, it allows the oppressor to create generalizations and stereotypes, usually negative, which are seen and accepted as normal by society at large.

During our second conversation, when Emilio and I talked about how some Latino boys were usually labeled as Mexicans, troublemakers, and lazy, I asked him if he was concerned when people labeled him Mexican. His response was "I don't want to be thought of like that because I believe I am trustworthy. I don't do any of those things. I feel like that's the wrong thing, I'd rather do the right thing." Tatum (1997) posits that when an individual perceives negative messages of the dominant group, he internalizes those messages that lead him to experience self-doubt and in extreme cases self-hate. Like many other Latino students, Emilio shared being afraid of people thinking of him like a trouble-making Mexican teenage boy.

In my teaching experience I witnessed how some Latino students avoided having any type of relationship with other Latino students, trying not to be labeled or targeted. Whether an individual conforms to the dominant culture or learns to resist it, experiencing an oppressive system is "physically and psychologically taxing" (Tatum, 1997, p. 26). During my observations in the cafeteria, I noticed that Julio, a light-skinned Colombian boy, never sat with other Latinos, but with white boys. I also noticed that in the classrooms he interacted mostly with white students. During our second conversation, I challenged him with some questions about it. I asked him who he usually sat with at lunch time. He commented that he usually sat with white people because those were his friends. Then I asked him why he did not like to hang out with other Latino or Mexican boys and he responded, "I guess I don't like Mexicans [He was laughing]. I mean not to hang out with them. Not that I don't like them, I just don't like to hang out with them. I don't know. I just don't know. It's nothing bad." I prompted him here and shared with him about

Latino teenagers not wanting to be labeled Latino and there were some times when we wanted people to understand that yes we were Latinos but we were different. He said, "Yes, each country is different. Here we are Hispanics but each country is different, culture is different, everything is different. It's the only thing is that we speak the same language." Although Julio's counterstory showed how he learned to internalize oppression against other Latino and/or Mexican boys, he shared during our first conversation how he also experienced being oppressed when his white peers referred to him as a drug dealer for being Colombian, "Oh, you're Colombian, so you sell drugs, 'cause Colombia has a reputation with cocaine." Portes and Rumbaut (2001) state:

> People whose ethnic, racial, or other social markers place them in a minority status in their group or community are more likely to be self-conscious of those characteristics. Youth may cope with the psychological pressure produced by such differences by seeking to reduce conflict and to assimilate within the relevant social context—the modal response of the children of European immigrants in the American experience. An alternative reaction may lead to the rise of reaffirmation of ethnic solidarity and self-consciousness. (pp. 151–152)

In his experience of feeling oppressed when people made derogatory comments about Colombians, Julio shared that not everybody was the same; however, he used his position as a Colombian boy with light skin, fluent in English, and his own agency to internalize discrimination against Mexican and other Latino boys.

Similarly, Emilio, a brown-skinned boy, born and raised in this country and whose parents emigrated from Cuba, shared that he preferred to have African American students as friends instead of whites or Latinos. Later, his counterstories unveiled how his choice related to issues of race/ethnicity, gender, class, and stereotype for being a Latino boy. He said:

> I don't feel good with them [whites and Latinos] ... I just feel odd. I don't really feel like I can fit with them like I fit with the others. There are so many different kinds of Latinos in school. I know a couple of Latinos that I do hang out a lot with because they are ... part of ... they know what they are doing.

Emilio argued that most Latino boys take things for granted at school. His hard work and commitment toward his education and goals pushed him to demand Latino peers that he considered "smart" and well behaved. He said, "They think before they act, I really like that about them." It seemed that Emilio's past experiences with some Latino students made him assume that most of them did not appreciate their education, "It's just the way they act in school. The way they speak in school." Emilio's counterstory also shows how he tried to avoid being labeled as uninterested about his education or as a troublemaker for being around other Latino boys. Being consciously aware of how his ethnicity and gender were used to stereotype Latino boys in school and his commitment toward his education led Emilio to feel more comfortable around Black boys. Like Julio's counterstory about being oppressed by his white peers, Emilio also shared how he once experienced being treated unfairly by a white peer because of his brownness.

> Emilio: I was going home with a friend … and … we were walking to his house and he told me to wait outside and he went inside and talked to his mom; he came back like "I'm sorry … I can't be out right now. My parents are fighting with me." I was kinda. I felt like it was me or my race or my skin color that affected that a little bit. He was white boy.
>
> R.V.:   Did you ask him about it?
>
> Emilio: I didn't really ask him about it because I didn't feel like; I didn't want him to know how I felt about it. I kinda just let it alone.

Emilio's experience showed how Latinos with brown skin are more vulnerable to experience discrimination because of their skin tone. Even though he realized his presence was questioned, he preferred to internalize that his friends' parents did not allow him to enter their house because he was Latino. Emilio's lack of association with other Latino and white boys showed how he, like Julio, internalized discrimination against white and Latino students. First, he internalized oppression against his own ethnic group by referring to them as disinterested in their education and then made generalizations about whites. He shared:

> A lot of whites can be arrogant and sometimes I feel like I don't need to be near that because that's too much and some of them are wealthier than I am and that makes me feel like an outcast, but the African Americans I sit with, they are there, they support me. They, they're just like me.

Strikingly, Emilio's comments showed how issues of race intersect with class. It is important to note how Emilio associates whiteness with better socioeconomic status when it relates to Communities of Color. Unfortunately, Emilio internalized that being an individual of color is synonymous with an inferior category within the societal structure. According to Suárez-Orozco et al. (2008), most immigrant children live in segregated neighborhoods and attend segregated schools; when they refer to their American friends, they usually mean the African American minority group. When I asked the other boys whom they sat with at lunch time, the rest of them shared that they sat primarily with Latino and Black boys. Carlos stated that he preferred to sit with Latino students because he knew where they came from and even though they did not look alike, he felt more related to them, "My best friend is Latino. He's also Dominican. We don't have lunch together. I sit with a group of Mexicans." José explained that he preferred to sit with other Latino boys because he was always afraid of not being able to be understood by the white boys since he was still learning English. He also admitted he hung out with Black students. He considered them more sociable. Tatum (1997) argues,

> The parts of our identity that do capture our attention are those that other people notice, and that reflect back to us. The aspect of identity that is the target of others' attention, and subsequently of our own, often is that which sets us apart as exceptional or "other" in their eyes. (p. 21)

Pedro and Luis hung out with all kinds of students since they both spoke English fluently. But they also admitted that they prefer to hang out with Latino boys because they felt more comfortable and they could speak English and Spanish or code switch in both languages. Pedro shared that while being with white boys he had to act smart so they did not look down on him. He said:

> Like with my white friends I am more ... not like serious ... but more intelligent not as goofy as I'm when I'm with my people because I feel like my friends ... like whites ... if you're not smart or like on their level then they look down on you, but with other ethnicities, friends, like everybody is like equal ... like you can be yourself more around them than you can be around other friends.

Tatum (1997) argues, "The dominant group holds the power and authority in society relative to the subordinates and determines how that power and authority may be acceptably used" (p. 23). Pedro recognized that in order to be accepted by his white peers he needed to engage in "smart" conversations. Otherwise, he would not be accepted. Few Latino teenage boys are able to conform to a culture of whiteness like Julio and Pedro. Others adopt oppositional identities, which are later used by school administrators, teachers, and school police officers to punish them.

There were instances when boys of color were not allowed to hang out at the local mall. Some of them were followed and kicked out of the mall by security officers just because of the color of their skin. José's counterstory also showed how he and his peers experienced discrimination as Latino boys and Spanish speakers at the local mall.

José:	Like at the mall. When I'm with my friends … most of them are Latinos … most of them born in Mexico … and then like … when I hang … when like we make five people in the group … then we start walking around … then the police kick us out because they think we are going to *robar algo* (steal something).
R.V.:	How do you feel about it?
José:	Bad … 'cause … I'm not that type of guy … and yeah … I don't know about my friends … but still.

José and his friends understood that he and his peers' presence at the mall represented a threat. Like José, most Latino boys and men who happen to be brown skinned and Spanish speakers internalized that society expects them to be shoplifters and violent. It is not unusual that in a culture of whiteness law enforcement officers (usually white men) interpret that when boys of color gather this is a sign of a potential riot or break-ins.

Profiling boys and men of color as a gender threat can lead them to internalize society's negative expectations of them. As a form of resistance and because of their age and gender, many Latino boys and men end up becoming what society expects them to be. Sadly, few of these young boys and men find positive mentors in their communities and schools that can help them navigate societal structures so they can avoid being victims of oppression and marginalization.

Many Latino/Latina students realize that their *Otherness* will always include questions with negative assumptions and generalizations based on their nationalities, skin color, and heritage languages. For instance, depending on *who* says *what* the word *Mexican* can be internalized as a racist slur, making somebody feel inferior. It can label him/her as illegal immigrant; it is easy to accept generalizations about Latinos, which usually are shaped by the media that portray brown-skinned Latino/Latina immigrants as illegal, poor, illiterate, and cheap laborers. Juan shared that some people believe that since he was Mexican, he will not graduate because many people say, "Mexicans don't care about school." Similarly, Pedro's counterstory revealed how he internalized the term "Hispanic" as homogenous and inferior when compared to the dominant group. He said:

Other people think that Hispanics don't try in school. Then they think since I'm Hispanic, that I'm not gonna do well in school which is like a standard because I'm a different color. I think sometimes like other ethnicities, they get advantage that I don't have ... like they get treated better because of their race ... like I have a disadvantage ... I have to work for it; other students because of their race, they don't really have to work hard because they're at a certain level because of their race. That's what I feel.

Pedro and Juan were also aware of an institutionalized racism against Latino immigrants, especially boys, just for being from a different race/ethnicity. Most of the boys in this book shared that in order to succeed in this country; they realized they had to work harder than white students in order to break the norm of Latino boys as potential dropouts. Likewise, Luis's counterstory also corroborated Pedro and Juan's narratives. He shared:

It was like way back in middle school. I remember the lady ... was a substitute and it was me and three other friends and we wanted to work together and she didn't let us and she let other kids work together ... and then she called the office down and she was like she had three Mexican boys disturbing in class.

It is important to note how teachers treated most Latino students as Mexican immigrants to this country, representing the *Other*. The teachers used these boys' Spanish language and skin tone to label them Mexicans. Why did the substitute refer to them as Mexican for having the ability to speak Spanish or for being brown-skinned? How did Luis and his friends internalize being called Mexican boys? The fact that they looked brown and could speak another language was apparently enough to label them Mexican. It is important to note how this substitute teacher used her position of power to refer to these boys' cultures and send a message of failure, which is most of the time internalized by most Latino/Latina children as *"it is the way it is."* In my years of teaching, I witnessed and read my students' stories of oppression and ridicule sometimes for speaking Spanish in the classroom to the point that some of them started imitating their teachers and peers by saying things like, "This is America, speak English or go back to Mexico."

Although the boys in this book narrated how they also experienced racism and other forms of subordination, their resiliency led them to develop a networking system that allowed them to navigate and to resist the dominant culture. Juan, who had a darker shade of brown and a Mesoamerican (indigenous) look, shared,

Some people say, "You're too dark" ... and ... it bothered me a little bit. I take pride of myself; I don't pull myself down because somebody said something about me. It's true about my skin color because I am a guy and all that stuff, but I don't let it hurt me because it's me.

Juan understood that his ethnicity and skin tone led him to be perceived as inferior to some other students at school; however, he used his cultural capital as a form of resiliency to overcome people's negative messages. Likewise, José said, "I mean for being Latino, *le echo más ganas a la escuela* (I work harder in school)." Both boys internalized that in school being Latino meant being less than the rest; however, José used his linguistic capital "*le echo más ganas a la escuela*" (I work harder in school) to remain in school. Although these boys built their own social and navigational capitals they also had to pay the cost of being aware of who they were within the dominant culture. The idea that they always represented the *Other* put them under a lot of psychological pressure since they had to cross imaginary borders to prove to the dominant group that they were also capable of doing good. However, these border-crossing experiences sometimes pushed them to risk their own cultural identities and sense of self in order to gain acceptance. Some students of color become consciously aware that if they failed within the culture of whiteness, they will end up being lumped or labeled bad students because of being Latino, Hispanic, or Mexican, so their failure will be accepted as the norm. But if they succeed or stand out in the dominant culture, their achievement is interpreted as part of the acculturation and assimilation processes.

Gender

> The challenges facing young men of color aren't purely education. The fact that many children come to school sick, hungry, without adequate housing or social and emotional support, and from families in distress makes the job of educating them much more difficult. (Noguera, 2012, p. 12)

Most Latino and Black boys are victimized in schools for resisting school colorblind structures, so they experience more punishment than any other boys. Because of issues of race, ethnicity, and class, they are not allowed to enjoy that freedom they are given as boys and men in their own communities. Instead, they are targeted and/or outcast as unmotivated about their education, troublemakers, gang members, lazy, and/or potential dropouts. Zamudio et al. (2011) argue that:

> At all levels of society, from schools to the criminal justice system, students of color, particularly boys, are perceived to be more threating, dangerous, and in need of more

discipline and harsher punishment often for the same infractions that, when committed by white students, would be dismissed with the sentiment that boys will be boys. (p. 108)

As a teacher in this school, I became aware of the pipeline from In-School-Suspension (ISS), to Out-of-School-Suspension (OSS) to school dropout or jail. I saw a lot of my former Latino boys being kicked out of the school for not following norms or becoming psychologically abused by culturally biased teachers and/or school authorities. I saw many Latino boys who, because of their age and lack of guidance, became victims of a culture of whiteness with low expectations and negative assumptions about them.

In this section I explore how these boys' experiences with punishment are related to their vulnerability of being targeted as boys of color. In addition, I also unpack how some teachers' comments about Latino boys challenged the participants' counterstories on punishment and the school culture of whiteness.

When I asked the boys who got punished more in school based on race, ethnicity, and gender, all of them agreed that Black and Latino boys got punished more frequently. First, Alex and Carlos agreed that Black and Latino boys got in trouble because they did not care about their education and their future. Carlos explained that some Black and Latino boys tended to emulate negative role models from TV, leading them to fall into stereotypes, "Because they say ... people are louder and stuff ... like they get into more trouble." Julio suggested that Black boys got in trouble because they want "to be funny." Tatum (1997) argues that when the targeted group internalizes the negative messages of the dominant group, it is very difficult for them to believe in their own ability. Certainly, these boys were emulating the dominant group by referring to Black boys as the victims or that Latino boys got in trouble because they imitated Black boys.

Asking the same question to teachers allowed me to validate how the school culture perpetuated colorblindness. Although most teachers agreed that Black and Latino boys got punished the most in school for breaking rules, resisting authorities, skipping, wearing saggy pants, or for cell phone use in class, they were not able to critically associate it to issues of oppression and marginalization towards boys of color. Instead, they perceived it as normalcy.

Ms. Dixon: I have to say that Black minorities are punished at a high rate than anyone else and it seems to be ongoing that once they get in trouble they seem to be kept in trouble whether for talking back or something.

Mr. Hunt: The majority of students who are punished may be Latino boys ... and Black males ... Latinos number one and Black males being number two ... that's just my observation. Part of it is probably people not being aware of the circumstances of backgrounds of those individuals ... and from the Latino boys stand point ... as far as being a macho type attitude and the same thing for Black African American males.

Mr. Moose: Probably the Black kids first, then the Latinos, and then white, usually boys.

None of the teachers were able to associate Black and Latino boys' punishment as being related to oppression for being boys of color. Only Mr. Hunt, who was the only African American teacher I talked to, mentioned the importance of knowing the boys' cultural and socio-economic backgrounds. Valenzuela (1999) posits:

> When real life concerns are thrust into the classroom, many teachers find themselves in uncomfortable and disorienting positions. They may be called on not only to impart their expert knowledge, but also to deal with barriers to students' learning of which they may not be fully aware or trained to recognize. (p. 74)

Strikingly, Mr. Sanchez's, Mr. Otto's, and Mr. Rivers's comments on punishment showed how these male teachers echoed issues of meritocracy, color-blindness, and culturally deficient model theory among minorities of color, especially boys. Schools act like packing factories, such that if one item does not fit the standards, he or she needs to be disposed of, which is usually through punishment. Mr. Sanchez said:

> I would say Black males are the ones who usually when you pay a visit to the ISS room [In School Suspension], there's usually one or two, no matter how small the group is ... at least half of them are Black males. I think it goes back to homes, I think. They come from broken homes where they are not raised by their parents and in some cases they are raised by their grandparents ... so I think those students come from broken homes.

It is important to highlight how Mr. Sanchez blamed Black boys and their "broken" families as the reasons why they misbehave in school. How does he know these boys come from "broken" homes? Is he saying that having both parents at home is a guarantee for boys' academic success? Or is he saying that grandparents do not know how to raise their grandchildren? Instead of finding out the reasons why these boys get punished, Mr. Sanchez used his privilege as light-skinned male teacher to make biased comments about Black boys and their families. In the end, he saw Black boys being punished as the norm, perpetuating a culturally deficient model in education. Mr. Otto commented:

> In particular boys sometimes try to bend the rules, dress code violation, maybe cellphone type violation … and then boys are … are challenged in terms of their reputation, school teachers and administrators have the tendency to buy back and obviously lead to repercussions … attendance wise it does seem too that minorities in school have problems with attendance, and I don't know the reasons why, but being that I cover ISS, I like to go through the write-ups and a lot of them are dress code violations and a lot of them are attendance issues, tardies, multiple absences or skipping, those type of things and those seem to be minorities and I don't know the reason why … I don't know why they are not going to class on time or not showing up to school on time for those reasons.

> African Americans and Hispanics … I don't feel our school in particular stereotypes and treats minorities different than the white students.

> Dress code violation … for one reason or another [he laughs] is seems like … African American and maybe Hispanic students like to … break dress code violation … I don't see a lot of white males with saggy pants, I see a lot of African Americans and some Hispanic boys with saggy pants and that's a particular rule that we try to correct at school … that's for boys, girls dress code violation is not usually an issue. That seems to be one that we try to clean up for a couple of years, and that seems to be one of them. Like I said I don't typically see white boys with saggy pants in our school … I don't know if it's just a trend … a fashion trend or what.

Mr. Otto's comments showed how boys of color are mostly punished for not following school rules. He also pointed out that minority students miss school more than white students, and that Black and Latino boys usually wore saggy pants in school. Suárez-Orozco and Suárez-Orozco (2001) state that teachers and school administrators often consider adolescent minority and immigrant boys as a threat. Hurtado, Haney, and Hurtado (2012) argue, "Clothing, hairstyle, and skin color register as social signifiers of the gang meta-identity. Any overt display of these characteristics place young Latino men at risk of state harassment" (p. 114). As a white man in a position of power as teacher, Mr. Otto had the privilege to remain oblivious as to why these young men of color were being punished. Unfortunately, schools systems in this country have been developed with a Eurocentric model and a system of inequity that pushes communities of color to conform to a culture of whiteness in order to access an education. It is important to note how Mr. Otto targeted Latino and Black students as rule breakers and as failures without recognizing how the school rules were structured to target students of color. He argued that the school did not treat minority students different than white students; however, the fact that more students of color were punished was indicative that boys of color's social and personal needs were not addressed appropriately at school. Instead, they were targeted and punished for not following a culture of whiteness. When boys, especially boys of color, do not have access to culturally relevant support from school, they tend to internalize their resistant behaviors as the norm even when they are aware of the negative consequences. Likewise, Mr. Rivers's comments reflected how punishing Black boys as rule breakers perpetuated racism. He added:

> I personally don't see inequity in the way discipline is handled in _____. I don't think that one group is pinpointed more than another. Now, in terms of who is punished more I don't believe it's the Whites or the Latinos, I believe would be the Blacks. That brings a completely different issue … that's probably … how can I put this … I think is because more frequently they are the ones that are breaking the rules and what that is a completely separate issue, I don't know but I feel like in terms of who's breaking the rules and who's being punished, I believe is proportional.

Ironically, Mr. Otto and Mr. Rivers, two white male teachers, did not see that the school segregated or targeted one group of student more than others. However, their comments on who gets punished more and the reasons why proved that if students do not conform to the school rules, boys of color, especially, become victimized. Even though Mr. Otto and Mr. Rivers agreed that the school treated all students fairly, their examples showed how experiences with punishment seemed to be the norm for bos of color. I argue that if Latino and Black boys represent the minority group in school, "Why do they get in trouble more than white boys for breaking the school rules? Why do school administrators and teachers choose not to associate this problem with race and gender issues? Why are Latino and Black boys tracked and targeted for breaking school norms that were created for a white and privileged group?" I posit that when schools punish boys of color for breaking school rules and nobody seems to critically analyze either the rules or punishment related to race and gender, Latino and Black boys then end up internalizing those messages of failure as boys and men of color as their only reality.

To encourage these boys to become actively engaged in the analysis portion of my book, I shared what a teacher (Mr. Otto) had commented on Blacks and Latinos as the only boys wearing saggy pants in school. The boys disagreed with the teacher's comments.

Luis:	Sometimes. Let say if somebody else says something. I guess you can say white and all that stuff … you know and they look decent and if you saw me like this [wearing PE clothes] they would probably say, "ah it is he who caused the trouble and not him [the white student.]"
Carlos:	They don't expect from a kid who is dressed up to do it.
Luis:	Say you see a white kid all dressed up, preppy like …
Carlos:	Uptight.
Luis:	And you see me like I am right now and they say, "Oh you probably did it."
R.V.:	They say it because you are a Latino boy?
Emilio:	For how you look.
Luis:	Yeah, for how you look, yeah I guess.
R.V.:	A teacher shared with me that he had never seen a white kid wearing saggy pants. That he only sees Black boys and Latino boys.
Luis:	I've seen white boys. [All of them start having side conversations about it.]
R.V.:	Is that true?
Luis:	I've seen white boys. I mean their shirts are long enough, so they can cover it and you can't tell, but I am pretty sure they are wearing it.
Emilio:	Also, teachers don't look at white boys as sagging because that has never been so often, but if you see a Black person going down the hallway, showing his underwear all out, and so they are expecting it all the time, so they don't really look at a White person who is probably sagging but they don't look at him. They do look at your race … that's what I think.

These boys' counterstories on dress code showed how the intersection of race, gender, and class were used to oppress them. They internalized how their way of dressing for being Latinos and poor made them more vulnerable than white boys. They knew that in order to fit in they not only had to behave but dress like white students. Emilio commented how teachers and school authorities sometimes made assumptions about students based on their race and ethnicity. This showed how these boys' struggles for survival and acceptance in school made them either adopt oppositional identities against a colorblind system or to conform to the system and develop issues of invisibility and dislocation representing the *Other*.

Noguera (2008) states that "in many schools, there may not be many explicit messages about race; but students receive implicit messages about race all the time that informs them what they think it means to be a member of a particular group" (p. 13). Hurtado et al. (2012) argue that young Latino boys are consciously aware when their appearance and behavior are interpreted through a dominant lens, labeling them as potential gang members, "on the verge of committing gang-related crimes" (p. 114). In their conversation, the boys realized that being a Black or Latino boy put them in a more visible position than being a white boy. They also mentioned how issues of class and skin color (phenotype) made them targets.

When talking to Juan about who got punished more at school based on race, ethnicity, and gender, Juan shared that when there was a white student and a Latino boy involved in a problem or class misbehavior, the Latino boy was usually singled out.

Juan: Well, usually if somebody gets in trouble is usually ... I think ... mostly ... horse playing around in class ... like I get in trouble a lot in class 'cause I'm usually horse playing, but then when it's something serious, they always blame me because I'm usually horse playing and it's not always me.

R.V.:   Why do you think that is?

Juan: Because like ... I was horse playing with a White girl and they thought it was me because I guess because she's white and I'm Mexican ... our race.

Luis and Pedro considered that white boys usually found the way to avoid being punished. I asked Luis to share any school experience in school when he felt treated unfairly for being a Latino boy.

Luis: I ... maybe last year ... I got in trouble for not showing up at the PE class, but I wasn't, I didn't come to school that day. I had three days of ISS ... and the kids I got wrote up with only got one and then went back to class the next day.

R.V.:   Were those kids Latinos too?

Luis: No.

R.V.:   Why do you think that is?

Luis: Because I've been in trouble before and they hadn't, maybe sometimes ... they let ... the white kids ... they let them go by more.

Pedro: I feel ... like ... like certain students; there's a white student and there's a Hispanic student. I feel like they would let the ... white student off of the warning and other kids get punished because of their race. I feel like they would do it again and they feel, they like the other kid will not do it again because they warned them. You see more Hispanics getting in trouble and Blacks than most white students and that kinda set the standards.

Juan's, Luis's, and Pedro's counterstories and the focus group conversation corroborated what most teachers commented on in their interviews. Most of the teachers agreed that Black and Latino boys got punished more than white boys; however, their lack of explicit attention to color contributed to the targeting of boys of color as a norm. Wise (2010) posits:

> Unfortunately, teachers often go out of their way to be colorblind or what educational theorist Mica Pollock calls "colormute"—by failing to discuss race, or even to use basic and benign racial descriptions to describe their students. As a result, educators replicate inequalities by failing to get to the bottom of their own biases on the structural impediments to equal opportunities within their schools. (p. 112)

What happens when minority students internalize that for being part of the minority group they are considered less or are more vulnerable than other boys in school? Since ethnicity and identity are social constructs shaped by the dominant culture, most minority youth experience psychological battles when they realize that their race/ethnicity and gender are used as negative frames of reference. These internal struggles are rarely seen by teachers and administrators, and only sometimes by parents. Some of them develop a sense of cultural pride, while some others experience *vergüenza* (shame) and sometimes rejection for being part of the minority group. Although the boys in this study agreed on being proud of their ethnic identities, there were some instances when they experienced feeling *vergüenza* (shame) due to their socio-economic status, ethnicity, or immigration status.

Internalizing Vergüenza (Shame)

> Then, like a flash, it became clear why Peggy stopped seeing me. I felt angry and insulted, but most of all, confused. I could not understand why anyone would not like us because we were Mexican. Mamá told us everyone was equal in the eyes of God and Papá told us we should respect everyone. (Francisco Jiménez in *Breaking Through*, 2001, p. 107)

When I asked these boys if they had ever felt *vergüenza* (shame), I realized this question was very personal. I soon learned that the word *vergüenza* had no space in their community cultural wealth since it is usually referred to as something negative or something that they knew existed but did not want to talk about unless they had developed a sense of *confianza* (trust). In order to develop that *confianza*, I explained to them that it was common for all of us to experience *vergüenza* for something, but that there was usually a turning point when individuals utilize their *vergüenza* as a stepping stone to develop a sense of *orgullo* (pride), closely associated to their community cultural wealth. I also shared that some people use their *vergüenza* to set goals in life or to resist oppression, injustice, poverty, and/or to develop a sense of hope for a better tomorrow. I aimed to push the boys to be reflective individuals on their own *vergüenza*, allowing them to unpack personal and familial experiences. Suárez-Orozco and Suárez-Orozco (2001) posits that although there were some gains for the children of immigrants who blended into the mainstream culture, they also had to pay the price of "unresolved shame, doubt, and self-hatred" (p. 106). He continues saying that race was a vital element in those gains for those children who looked white, like the mainstream; however, it is not the case with today's immigrants of color whose skin color make them the *Other*. I found that these boys' counternarratives on *vergüenza* shared three common threads related to class, immigration status, and ethnicity.

Lack of Money

Alex and Pedro commented that lack of money always made them feel ashamed. They said that seeing their mothers and siblings struggling financially caused them to feel uncomfortable. Even though they were teenagers, they had already developed a moral responsibility for their parents and younger siblings. Suárez-Orozco et al. (2008) agree that immigrant families take immigration as a "familial project" where everybody in the family has a responsibility. Parents work hard to make sure their children have better opportunities in the future and children are expected to support parents around the house. In some instances, when the father is absent, it is usually the boy(s) who perform(s) the father figure role in the family.

Alex: Because ... my mom and my sister are, are right now the only ones working besides me. So ... back then I couldn't do nothing about 'cause well my dad will send money to help us pay for the bills but still we wouldn't have enough money so we could buy a lot of groceries like we needed. So we were on a tight budget I guess and now I work, I have, I pay the water bill, I pay our internet bill and I give money to my mom so she can buy groceries or whatever.

R.V.:   How does that make you feel?

Alex: I mean, I feel like ... that's the least I can do, I'm, I'm still living there.

R.V.:   Do you feel that's more like an obligation?

Alex: I don't feel like, uh, because she doesn't ask me to do it. I'll just do it because I can, because it's helping out my family.

Alex's statement ran counter to the teachers' narratives about Latino boys' lack of motivation, not caring, and breaking rules. It is not that Alex does not care about his education. As a young man, Alex internalized a moral obligation to support his mother and siblings. It is very common that within Latino families, boys and men, who have seen their mothers suffering due to the absence of a masculine figure or lack of money, decide to sacrifice their education and get a job to contribute to the family's expenses. In addition, his lived experiences as a gang member exposed him to having to cope with society and school obstacles. When boys experience any type of oppression in society, which is also institutionalized in the school culture, their education is not seen as a way to obtain social upward mobility. On the contrary, most of them end up internalizing their social conditions. As a result, the fact that most of them end up getting in trouble, dropping out, and getting a low-paid job become normalcy.

Pedro's counterstory on not having money is similar to Alex's. He felt a moral obligation to find a job so he can support his mother and pay some bills. Culturally, most Latin Americans, especially those coming from working-class backgrounds develop a sense of family responsibility associated with familial capital where individuals support their parents and younger siblings as a way of thanking them for their sacrifice when they were growing up. By helping younger siblings, the immigrant youth also passes on the familial capital to a new generation. Suárez-Orozco and Suárez-Orozco (2001) agree:

> Among many adolescents, success in school means not only self-advancement and independence, but also, and perhaps even more importantly, making parental sacrifices worthwhile by "becoming a somebody." For such youth, "making it" may involve "giving back" to parents, siblings, peers, and other less fortunate members of the community. (p. 113)

Pedro's *vergüenza* takes place when the dominant culture stereotypes Latino families as poor and views "poor" as being related to bad people rather than a result of a system of oppression. He said:

> Probably the financial part because my parents are both divorced so I live with my mom, and dad usually does not give her money and sometimes we have to go without stuff. It makes me feel bad about my mom because she has to pay for everything. And my sister doesn't live with us anymore. [His sister got pregnant at a young age and moved out of the house with her boyfriend.] It is just me and my younger sister. Sometimes we need stuff and sometimes I feel like I should get a job to help her financially pay for some of my expenses so she doesn't have to deal with it. And I don't know; it makes me feel bad. Some people think Hispanics don't like ... like they're poor; they don't like, they don't have a lot. It's kind of embarrassing; a little, like I feel a

little embarrassed sometimes, like I cannot have things my friends have. Like some of them have nice things.

This counterstory shows what I analyzed previously about labels and how they hurt individuals. In his comments, Pedro believed that being Hispanic was seen as a synonym of poverty. Also, the fact that his father left the family and his sister got pregnant pushed him to internalize social generalizations and stereotypes placed on Communities of Color in this country. Suárez-Orozco et al. (2008) argue that since poverty is recognized as a significant risk factor in education, poor children become more vulnerable to experience "psychological distress, affecting their concentrating and sleeping, anxiety and depression" (p. 90).

Undocumented Status

One of the biggest obstacles some Latino/Latina students have to cope with relates to their immigration status in this country. Although most of them attend schools with aspirations of upward social mobility, this dream becomes a myth when they realize that because of their legal status, they cannot get any type of financial aid to support their higher education. Being undocumented in this country leads many Latino/Latina teenagers to feel *vergüenza*, especially when their peers, teachers, and school counselors ask them about their futures after high school. In this section, I unearth how these boys' counterstories on *vergüenza* voice the internal battle that many undocumented Latino/Latina students deal with in this country. José commented:

> Not really 'cause there is this like … there is a lot of Mexicans and stuff and … [thinking] I don't know. Like if you say something about their country all the Mexicans will start picking on you. And porque te debe dar vergüenza de dónde vienes. [I prompted him with some examples.] Immigration status … [he didn't have a clear picture of the term immigration status, so I prompted him again] kinda … [he was thinking so deeply] like for example si voy al college y no me reciben porque [if I go to college and they don't accept me because] I don't have papers y si reciben a mi amigo que si tiene papeles me va a dar un poco de vergüenza [and if they accept my friend who has papers, I will feel ashamed]. I don't know why, but a mi me daria [I will feel that way].

Juan said:

> My immigration status … There is all people always talking about, they took driver's ed and they got their permit and stuff and I get sad and whatever because I can't get it, because I wasn't born here. And usually you have to be born here to get all that stuff. And is … something with me that … is not good.

Although José's and Juan's comments on their immigration status made them feel ashamed and sometimes frustrated, they developed resiliency while building up a network orientation (Stanton-Salazar & Spina, 2000). They learned how to seek positive support from available adults. This network orientation from positive adults and competent peers allowed them to cope with their immigration situation. José used soccer to develop his own social and navigational capitals, while Juan's network system developed at the local library. Unfortunately, it is not always the case with some undocumented students, especially boys, who decide to drop out once they realize they cannot pursue higher education or get a decent job once they finish high school. Instead, they end up joining their parents, relatives, or friends in factories, construction sites, or landscaping.

Ethnicity

The absence of Latino/Latina adults in leadership positions at the schools pushes some Latino/Latina students to feel *vergüenza* about their ethnicity. Some students become aware of white privilege when they realize that most of their teachers and school administrators are white or when they represent the only non-white student among their peers, especially if they are taking advanced or college courses. Others internalize that because of their cultural backgrounds their chances to succeed in life are more difficult or nonexistent. In this section, I unpack how Carlos, Emilio, and Julio's *vergüenzas* were related to their ethnicity.

Carlos:	I used to be ashamed of being Hispanic because it seems that white people have more privileges than Hispanics ... like big people in this country are usually white. I think there's only one judge in the Supreme Court that's Hispanic. Most of them are white; the governor is white ... like this is harder for a Hispanic person to be at the top than it is for a white person. That's why I used to feel ashamed but not anymore. Now I think that being Hispanic is not *gonna* stop me from being what I want to be in the future.
R.V.:	What was the turning point?
Carlos:	Just seeing other role models ... other Hispanics ... don't care about The odds of being Hispanic ... I look up to that.

The fact that Latino students, like Carlos, did not see their group in leadership positions in society and school also affected their individual identities. Students of color often do not see their people developing positive or leadership roles in society. Instead, they see in the media that boys and men of color are shown as criminals, drug dealers, or abusive parents, leading them to adopt these behavioral patterns as being a real man. In my experience at this school, I was the only Latino male teacher in the school. Later, the administration hired two Latina teachers who taught Spanish. Then they hired two Latino males to teach ESL. Even though the school had few Latino teachers, most of us had to learn to conform to school structures of inequity and inequality.

Emilio: Yeah … sometimes when I am around a different kind I am, such as Caucasians, sometimes I feel I don't belong there because usually I feel like a third wheel. If you understand that, I feel embarrassed because I am the only one that is not talking or stuff like that.

Julio: Okay maybe … here … you know how many people are racist here … and I guess you go out and somebody is more rude to you 'cause of your skin I guess; like they don't treat you the same, maybe at a store or a restaurant or something.

Although Carlos, Emilio, and Julio were able to make use of their navigational and social capitals, they still struggled to blend in with the dominant group. Even though they all spoke English, they also shared how they experienced being "a third wheel," "ashamed for being Hispanic," or being targeted for being Latinos.

These boys' counterstories with *vergüenza* were related to issues of lack of money, undocumented status, and ethnicity. Voicing these boys' internal shame demonstrates that schools as democratic institutions are not fulfilling their purpose. Schools are mirroring our communities and society where Communities of Color are still marginalized and segregated. Although these boys shared three reasons for experiencing *vergüenza*, I claim that their shame for being poor, undocumented, and for being Latino was closely related to issues of colorblindness. Latino boys' experiences with racism and discrimination push them sometimes to become resistant, unmotivated, and finally to drop out of school. Some of those who stay reject their own peers in order to fit in or to avoid being associated with negative issues of nationality, class, language acquisition, or immigration status; while others, like these boys, decide to overcome their *vergüenza*, become resilient, and stay in school without losing their cultural/ethnic identities.

Conclusion

In this chapter, I used *Latinidades* to explore how these boys' commonalities as Latinos were also punctuated by distinctions based on class, immigration status, heritage language, and skin color. All participants, however, agreed that preserving their Spanish language allowed them to communicate with their parents, relatives, and friends. They also suggested that being bilingual allowed them to earn more money. Unfortunately, the lack of a serious Spanish curriculum did not prepare these boys to become fully bilingual citizens. Sadly, these students will probably end up forgetting their heritage languages with the meritocratic idea that in order to succeed in this country, immigrants have to speak only in English. Tatum (1997) argues that some immigrant students experience linguistic discrimination for speaking their heritage languages, leading them to internalize rejection to experience a positive sense of identity. Zamudio et al. (2011) claim that

> English-only instruction sends the message to whites that their language and, by extension, their culture, is more valuable and superior to that of others. They come to see their English proficiency as a natural state of affairs that also legitimates a distinct advantage. Their social status is high because their language status is high. (p. 61)

A serious curriculum should teach Spanish-speaking students to develop cultural pride for their language, a curriculum where they can not only study their language, but also learn about literature, art, music, philosophy, religions, and other cultural groups. Solórzano and Yosso (2009) posit that dominant studies have always claimed that for students of color to experience American success, they need to give up their heritage language by "loosening or cutting family and community ties" (p. 31). Contrary to what majoritarian assumptions and dominant ideologies promote, many scholars (Cammarota, 2008; Delgado Bernal, 1998, 2002; Fernández, 2002; Garcia, 2001; Noguera 2008, 2012; Noguera & Yonemura Wing, 2006; Solórzano & Yosso, 2009 Stanton-Salazar, 1997, 2001; Stanton-Salazar & Spina, 2000; Suárez-Orozco & Suárez-Orozco, 2001; Suárez-Orozco et al., 2008; Valenzuela, 1999; Yosso, 2006a, Yosso, 2006b) support the idea(s) that language is an important part of an individual's culture and identity. I argue that teachers, school administrators, staff, and other stakeholders need to understand that the teaching and preservation of the Spanish language as a cultural capital will allow Latino students to develop a global identity needed in today's world where the English language can no longer be taken as the key language to obtain academic success and social upward mobility.

In the previous chapter these boys shared that an individual's academic success was not based on ethnicity. Instead, they agreed it depended on how hard a student worked to achieve it. However, during the rest of this book, these boys told of how racism, gender discrimination, and class became obstacles for them to achieve academic success. In addition, teachers' comments on Black and Latino boys' behavioral problems and frequent punishment proved how race, gender, and class issues influence Latino boys' experiences in the school. Teachers' colorblindness and meritocratic ideas, as well as culturally biased comments about Latino boys, did not allow them to understand how racism and gender discrimination operated in the school.

Another salient point relates to the pan-ethnic labels and how they affect Latino students. Students of color, in this case Latino boys, are trapped under the umbrella of "at risk," "No Child Left Behind," or "Race to the Top." No matter how hard they work as individuals, when schools blanket their academic performance as the Latino/Hispanic sub-group, they end up joining the pool of disadvantaged. If some of them succeed academically, they still become an anomaly since they do not represent the norm. This colorblind system does not allow teachers, administrators, and counselors to realize how some students of color internalize the idea that their ethnic identity and heritage language represent drawbacks for them to succeed within the dominant culture. What teachers and school administrators need to recognize is the impact colorblindness shapes in every aspect of the school, from the school curriculum to how they involve these boys' parents in their education. School systems have to develop a school curriculum where students of color can see their group represented not only as part of history but as current and active members of this society. Students of color have the right to become active participants of their own cultural identities; they are entitled to discuss how different forms of subordination are still practiced in their neighborhoods and perpetuated in their schools. They can no longer be passive learners who accept multiple layers of oppression as norms. Latino/Latina students need to learn how the intersection of their race/ethnicity, gender, and other social categories impact their *Otherness*.

· 5 ·

EL MUERTO Y EL ARRIMA'O
AL TERCER DÍA APESTA
(THE DEAD BODY, AS WELL AS THE
GUEST, STINKS BY THE THIRD DAY)

Latino immigrants and their children are struggling to gain a foothold in American society in the face of governmental policies that make their lives exceeding difficult. The immigration status of themselves or their parents makes getting an education, a job, a driver's license, and medical care both a daily effort and something that requires the development of long-term strategies. (Chavez, 2008, p. 50)

One morning my students and I were analyzing some *dichos* (proverbs) in Spanish, how some of them had English translations, and how some others were strictly related to our Latin American cultures. Suddenly, a Latina girl exclaimed: *"El muerto y el arrima'o al tercer día apesta"* (The dead body, as well as the guest, stinks by the third day). Since I had already heard that *dicho* (proverb) back home, I asked my student how it related to us as immigrants to this country. She shared that this *dicho* (proverb) applied to racist people who did not like Latinos/Latinas. My student's example became a form of communal knowledge for everyone in the room. Whether through personal experiences or those of family members, there was a collective consensus that discrimination was something we had to face on a daily basis. We became consciously aware that Latino/Latina immigrants were not welcome in the community.

Since many community members (Latinos and local leaders) happened to know me for my jobs as teacher, leader, and freelance writer for a Spanish newspaper, I had many good opportunities to engage in informal dialogues within the community. When I went to the gym one afternoon, a young Latino man, who used to work for a well-known furniture factory plant, shared with me how he and his peers felt at their work place. He said: "They [whites] only want us when we are in the factory working, but after that they want us to disappear." This man with little or no formal education understood how racism and segregation operated at his workplace and the community. He knew that Latino workers were needed when hard work was required but after that, they became invisible and unwanted.

When Race and Ethnicity Intersect Immigration, Class, and English-Language Acquisition

> They talked about Mexicans. When a lady with a goiter said that Mexicans were pretty trustworthy, especially with orders, if you talk to them really slowly, a Mexican man stood up angrily and yelled at the woman. He said that was Fresno's problem: White people only saw Mexicans as manual laborers. (From *Jesse* by Gary Soto, 1994, p. 14)

In this chapter, I unearth how these boys' parents' counterstories with issues of immigration, class, and language acquisition become a common language by most immigrants of color in this country. I unveil how these social issues keep these boys and their families trapped in *caste minority status* (Ogbu, 2004), what I refer to as *círculo de pobreza* (circle of poverty). Ogbu claimed that immigrant minorities achieve success because they are not aware of how systems of oppression apply to them, and *caste minorities* (African Americans) are consciously aware of their reality in which they live. Contrary to Ogbu's assertion, Valdés (1996) found in her study with Mexican families that Mexican immigrants can also be considered part of the *caste minority* group in the United States when they:

> Become conscious that they are no longer like Mexican nationals who have remained in Mexico, feel little identification with these Mexican nationals, self-identify as "Americans," become aware that as persons of Mexican origin they have low status among the majority society, and realize the permanent limitations they will encounter as members of this group. (p. 26)

Even though there is some validity in Valdés's argument about the Mexican group, it is important to highlight that it is sometimes problematic to make generalizations about experiences of Mexican immigrant families since they represent a heterogeneous group. Some Mexican families have been living in this country for generations and consider themselves as the first settlers while some other families have recently arrived legally or without legal documentation (Valdés, 1996, p. 24). Like many Mexican individuals, Latin American immigrants arrive to this country representing rich and diverse groups, who are then labeled as Latino or Hispanic. Vazquez (2000) says:

> Even within Hispanic populations from the same country of origin, there can be differences in beliefs, customs, and values that are shaped by such factors as family background, recency of immigration, degree of acculturation, regional concentration, level of educational attainment, income, and English language proficiency. ("Implications," para. 4)

Even though there is a general myth of coming to the United States to achieve "The American Dream" or "a better life," some Latino/Latina immigrants end up in this country by choice while some others flee from their countries due to political conflicts, war, or natural disasters. As Portes and Rumbaut (2001) state:

> Whether prompted by the need to escape political persecution at home or by the urge to seek a better life for oneself and one's family, the motivations of immigrants converge in a remarkable way as they reach U.S. shores: to survive in any manner possible and then to move ahead, seeking all the possible support mechanisms, the open and hidden avenues for mobility that a complex, advanced society makes available. The streets of America may be paved with gold, but for newcomers that promise quickly becomes an aspiration rather than a reality. The country seldom makes its wealth easily accessible. Instead, it demands hard toil and much ingenuity for newcomers, and it can throw obstacles, sometimes unsurpassable, in the path of some of them. (p. 71)

In the following counternarratives, I explore how these boys' and their parents' immigration journeys, socioeconomic status before and after coming to this country, and a lack of English language acquisition lead most Latino/Latina families to join a *cast minority status*.

Immigration Stories

> I call myself Puerto Rican, but I think ... I think I'm, I'm American. I know I'm American, but if somebody asks me, I tell them that I'm Puerto Rican first—Raúl

During my experience as a teacher and community leader I learned from students, parents, and friends that some Mexican and Central American families entered the country illegally escaping social issues such as poverty, persecution, and drug-related violence; others arrive in the United States to reunite with their parents and/or other relatives after many years of separation. Some are in debt even before they arrive here. I heard and read their stories of how most of them have to find a job to pay back whoever brought them here; otherwise, they become victims of death threats and harassment, including to their relatives back home, while others spend years saving their earnings to pay a "coyote" (human smuggler) to bring the rest of the family to join them.

Some of the students in my book were born and raised in this country, while some others were brought here as infants or young children. Some of them recalled their immigration journeys and some others learned it through their parents. Regardless of how these boys learned how they or their parents immigrated to this country, it is important to note that immigration was internalized as part of their community cultural wealth, which was later on used to develop resiliency to survive and to navigate the American system.

Immigration from Mexico

In the following counterstories, three boys explain how their parents crossed the border from Mexico to come to the United States. Their narratives show how painful the experiences were, not only physically but also psychologically; these stories shaped their lives as immigrants and as teenage boys. It is important to note that Luis was born and raised in this country and Juan and José crossed the Mexico-U.S. border when they were little.

When I asked Luis how his parents came to this country, he said, "Like any other person [human smuggler]. They crossed the border." Interestingly, Luis internalized that every Latin American or Mexican immigrant crossed the border illegally. This also shows how some individuals are not even aware that there is a legal option to immigrate because it is literally out of reach for most of them. Since Juan came to this country when he was still a little boy, all he remembered was pretty vague or what his parents shared with him.

R.V.:	Do you remember how you came here?
Juan:	I don't really know; I was so little. A desert, you have to walk a desert, carry water and stuff ... I think you have to swim and something. My parents carried me; my dad carried me.
R.V.:	Do you know how long it took them?
Juan:	I am not sure I think it was a day or two. Because I knew someone who was crossing over, he got deported back to El Salvador, so he was

coming back and a *coyote* [human smuggler] brought him over and
they took him in California.

R.V.:   Did you come all the way from California?

Juan: Yeah. Some of my siblings were already here, but my mom came here
with my dad and they worked some and my mom used to send money
to my grandma. My dad brought me here. I stayed home [in the U.S.]
for two years before I started going to school here.

Like Juan's parents, many poor and lower-middle-class Mexican families
crossed the border illegally to look for a better future for their children or to
escape social inequality and poverty in their countries. During the first years,
most of these immigrant families send money back home to support the relatives who are taking care of their children, just as Juan's parents sent money
to his grandmother who was caring for him in Mexico.

When I asked José about his immigration experience to this country, I
understood that he did not have a clear picture of how long he, his mom, and
brother waited back in Mexico before they joined his father who was already
living and working here. José's counterstory narrated how he was reunited
with his father after living with his grandparents back in Mexico until he was
eight years old.

José: It was awesome and stuff 'cause the only person I used to call dad was
my grandfather. And then it was nice and awesome for me to like …
to have my real dad, like in person and stuff.

R.V.:   How was it meeting your father after so long?

José: It was like start over again.

R.V.:   Have you asked your father why he left you and your mother?

José: No, 'cause I knew … my mom was telling me why 'cause of the econ-
omy problems and I kinda see it … I mean I didn't hate him and stuff
'cause he used to call us mostly every day … he used to send me money
for my parties and stuff so I kinda loved him. I was never against him
and stuff. My dad *me mandaba dinero para que yo creciera bien* (used to
send money so I could be brought up well).

José's narrative shows how some immigrant families reunite after years of being
separated as a result of their immigration to this country. It took many years
for José and the rest of this family to be reunited with his father. He shared
during this interview that at first he did not recognize his father since he left
home when he was still a little boy. José had to relearn to refer to his biological father as dad since he always called his grandfather "papa" (dad) back in
Mexico. In his counterstory, he also shared how his mother taught him the

reasons why his father immigrated to this country and how his father sent money back home to support his education, clothes, and parties. It is important to highlight how José's counterstory also challenges deficit perceptions of Mexicans and other Latinos not caring about their families or education. Jose's father's sense of family responsibility was evident when he sent money back to support his family. He had to save a lot of money to pay for his family to reunite with him in this country.

Immigration from Cuba

Cuban immigration to the United States increased dramatically after Fidel Castro's revolution in 1959. The first immigrants were light-skinned, wealthy, educated, affluent, and well received Cubans who left the island the first days of the revolution. Many of them were able to bring their personal wealth with them and created businesses in the United States (Tatum, 1997). The second wave of Cuban individuals came from the lower socioeconomic status and was not as fortunate. Portes and Rumbaut (2001) claim,

> The Cuban government's decision to open the port of Mariel to all Cubans wishing to leave the island triggered a chaotic exodus that brought over 125,000 refugees in a six-month period, more than the sum total of the preceding eight years. The image of the Mariel boats bringing thousands of ragged refugees onto American shores was transmitted nationwide by the media and instantly altered public opinion about Cubans. The increasingly restrictive official policy culminated in the 1994 decision by the Clinton administration to turn back all Cuban boats and rafts found at sea. (p. 262)

Tatum (1997) supports the claims by Portes and Rumbaut (2001), noting that "Marielitos" were "typically much poorer, less educated, and darker-skinned than earlier refugees" (p. 136). However, this policy did not stop Cubans from leaving the island to reach the United States, shores. Emilio said:

> It was a little bit planned ahead of time. They already knew how to get here but the problem was the money … what they did; they talked to a guy who had a boat but he wouldn't use it for fishing, he would use it to transport people from the island to the U.S. And what they did, they made a deal with him that when they get their overtime they would pay him the money that they owed. And so he made the deal with them and … then he brought them over the U.S. and they encountered a couple problems; they encountered the U.S. Coastal Guard and my mother was pregnant of me and she got stuck in a cabinet, a little cabinet under the boat with probably thirty people. She said it was really crowded, she couldn't breathe. They've got to hide at the time. That happened a couple of times and from then they just got here.

During this conversation, I noticed how Emilio internalized his parents' journey and difficulties in this country. He always referred to his hard work as a way to pay his parents back for what they did for him and his siblings. Many immigrant families use their journey stories as a cultural asset to instill in their children hard work and to take advantage of living and studying in this country; however, some of these immigrant children do not find the same type of support at schools.

Immigration from Dominican Republic

Dominicans represent the largest-scale immigration to the United States. During the regime of President Rafael Leonidas Trujillo, few upper and middle-class Dominicans received exit visas to leave the island: "Compared to the 9,897 Dominicans whose destination was the U.S. in the 1950s, the number in the 1990s was closer to 335,000" (Campos, 2013, p. 77). Most Dominicans live in the urban areas of New York, New Jersey, Florida, Massachusetts, and Pennsylvania (U.S. Census Bureau, 2010).

Carlos, whose parents came from the island while they were still very young, was born and raised in New Jersey. He shared,

> I don't remember that much but my mom; mom came to the U.S. when she was twelve years old. My grandfather wanted a better job, a better life for his kids, so they all got paper and got over here, got citizenship to all of his kids, he and his wife. And my father, I know he had a really hard time in the Dominican Republic, he said he was the only boy out of six sisters. He had to work for everything he had to do, everything he wanted, nobody gave him anything. He had to work his whole life. And when he came to America, he married my mom and he got his papers.

Carlos's story reflects what many poor or lower-middle-class people experience in this country. Even though his grandparents immigrated here first many years ago and brought his mother at a young age, they became part of a caste minority group. His father, because of his lack of education and legal documentation, worked in a pizzeria while his mother was unemployed. I will discuss this in depth in the next section.

Carlos's and Emilio's cultural backgrounds and immigration stories (Cuba and Dominican Republic) brought to my study the voices of two Caribbean teenage boys whose immigration stories and cultures are usually silenced by the labels Latino, Hispanic, and the common misperception that all Latinos are Mexican.

Immigration from Central and South America

Central and South American immigrants also leave their lands because of war, natural disasters, political problems, and/or for economic reasons in search of better opportunities. Because of their immigration status, illiteracy skills in English and sometimes their native languages, most of these immigrants, especially men, end up joining the poor and working class in this country. This pool of underpaid individuals sometimes includes well-educated Latino/Latina immigrants who had no choice but to leave their countries because of civil wars, natural disasters, political problems, and/or better economic opportunities (Campos, 2013; Menjivar, 2005; Tatum, 1997). Because of the closeness to the United States, some poor and lower-middle-class Central American individuals and families risk their lives coming to this country looking for better jobs to support themselves and their relatives back home.

Pedro's parents moved from El Salvador to California first; then they decided to move south looking for a better environment to raise their children. Like many immigrants, Pedro's parents moved to the United States for economic reasons. He shared:

> I think my dad; he was little when he came here to California. My mom, she was there [El Salvador] until she was 18. I think she worked there like after she graduated from high school she worked in a factory. And then she came over here ... and then she didn't work.

As an immigrant, I have experienced how difficult it is to visit or to move to this country. After paying a large amount of money (starting at $160 per person for a tourist visa) for an interview at the U.S. Embassy, most individuals are denied a visa due to lack of financial resources, educational background, and sometimes for breaking the law in their native countries. Julio was born in Colombia and brought to this country when he was two years old. He shared how he and his parents first arrived to this country:

Julio:	They [his parents] decided to come to the US to work ... yes, to work ... have a better life.
R.V.:	Do you know how they came here?
Julio:	Visa. They got a tourist visa.
R.V.:	How long have you been here?
Julio:	Thirteen years. I was two years old when I came here.
R.V.:	When you came here, did you come with your parents?

Julio: No, they came here first and then we came with my cousins' grandma, my mom's cousin's grandma. My parents were already here, and we stayed back like a couple of months and then he [his father] went.

Like Julio's parents, many immigrants from all over the world come to this country with a tourist visa. Many who come visit this country then decide to adopt the United States as their new home, assuming that getting a job or making decent money will allow them to fulfill their dream of *una vida mejor* (a better life) for them, their children, and their loved ones back home. As a result, most of them end up overstaying their tourist visas, thus making them undocumented immigrants. Portes and Rumbaut (2001) claim that even though some immigrants possess credentials that allow them to reach upper social mobility it does not guarantee success "because the transfer of credentials does not occur in a vacuum but in the context set by the way immigrants and their families are received" (p. 72). The reality is that the majority of them, many highly educated and middle-class individuals, end up earning low-wage salaries since they cannot obtain the legal documentation (social security number) or credential transfers that can allow them to apply for better and/or decent jobs. Instead, most of them get two or three jobs, working long hours in order to survive the cost of living in the U.S. Many Latino/Latina immigrants, especially on the bottom of their social strata, are the ones paying the consequences of U.S. imperialism and capitalism in Latin American countries. In the case of Mexico, Cuadros (2006 explains:

In the 1990s, the U.S. passed the North American Free Trade Agreement with the idea that free trade between the U.S., Canada, and Mexico would help the economies of all participating countries. The agreement ended up being a disaster for the Mexican farmer. It allowed heavily subsidized U.S. corn and other agri-business products to be dumped into Mexico. Millions of Mexican farmers could no longer compete against these artificially lower prices and many were forced to leave their farms ... Not being able to work in urban communities, they migrated north into the U.S. where they found jobs in the meatpacking and poultry-processing industries. (pp. vii–viii)

In my trips to Mexico as a community leader, I witnessed how many Mexican farmers decided to leave their lands after they learned that commercial agreement was a failure. I also learned that after U.S. companies started shutting down cheap-labor factories in Mexico and Central American countries, people were encouraged by their former employers, friends, and other relatives to immigrate to this country to find jobs and a better future. Unfortunately, most of those immigrant families, who come with the idea of making better salaries and futures, end up joining a minority-status category by making low-wages in working-class jobs that no others want, pushing them to get trapped in poverty.

Trapped in Poverty

Immigrant families' socioeconomic and educational backgrounds determine the child's experiences and opportunities in schools. (Suárez-Orozco & Suárez-Orozco, 2001, p. 128)

Wise (2010) argues that children of color and their families often live in segregated communities where rates of poverty are higher than the rest of their communities. He continues on to say that because many generations of Black and Latino families have suffered housing discrimination, their children are victims of double discrimination due to economic and racial marginalization in their communities and then in the schools. Suárez-Orozco et al. (2008) add that color is not the only pattern used to segregate students of color, but poverty and linguistic isolation create a so-called "triple segregation." They suggest that these types of segregation are linked to negative educational outcomes such as lower achievements, school violence, and higher dropout rates. In the previous theme, these boys narrated their parents' immigration journeys to this country looking for a better future and opportunities for their children, especially a better education. However, many new immigrant families ignore how their race/ethnicity, educational backgrounds, immigration, and socioeconomic status keep them trapped for generations.

In order to discuss how issues of class shaped these boys' experiences in education, I unpack their parents' educational backgrounds and socioeconomic status before immigrating to the U.S. Once in this country, I unveil how most Latino/Latina immigrant families still live in poverty, working long hours, having multiple jobs, and making low-wage salaries. Like most Communities of Color, most Latino/Latina immigrant families get trapped at the bottom of the U.S. societal structure. Alex shared:

> My mom got her like, the basic studies that they need, that they do in Guatemala, and so did my dad, but my dad told me he had been working since he was like 13 and my mom would help her mom around the house. My father was just doing little jobs like cutting grass and taking care of animals like cattle, they have a lot of cattle over there.

Alex's parents did not attend school since they lived in a village in rural Guatemala where most people live on farms and raise livestock. Along with poverty is the lack of education that many Latino/Latina immigrants share in this country, especially those from rural Mexico, Central America, and the Caribbean. In my experience as an educator and observations during leadership trips to some villages in Mexico, I learned that many parents did not have access to formal education in their home communities. Others possessed a basic third- or fifth-grade education, while others were totally illiterate or spoke indigenous languages as their only way to communicate. The fact that most of these parents come to this country to work and to support their children and other relatives back home makes it almost impossible for them to obtain an education here. Instead, they prefer to focus on their families' well-being and allow their children to get a formal and better education. Carlos shared that his mother came here when she was 12 years old and completed her high school education in New York. His father came from the Dominican Republic to work when he was an adolescent. He commented, "My father, I don't think he even entered high school because he had to work since he was a child, so he never went to school. My mom, she's a high school graduate." Carlos shared that since his father was the only boy in the family, he was expected to work to support his parents and younger siblings, which meant that getting an education was not a priority in his family. During our second interview, Carlos shared that when his father moved from the island to this country, he was undocumented for some years until he married Carlos's mother and then legalized his status. Although Carlos's mother graduated from high school in this country, she did not have enough schooling to obtain a decent job. The last time I interviewed Carlos, he told me that his mother had been laid off from a local factory and was looking for a new job.

Due to the communist system and poverty in Cuba, Emilio's parents had to work in the field picking up crops before they decided to move to this country. He said:

> They [his parents] really *kinda* do a lot … my dad was drafted to the military because when you are seventeen you have to be and that was really bad because he had to come a different way here [U.S.]. They only used to pick up rice for my grandfather. My mom did the same thing my dad did. Both worked on the same field, picking up rice. They dropped out probably around junior year, eleventh grade and that's when they came.

Even though Emilio's parents risked their lives while trying to abandon the island, they preferred to leave everything behind in order to start a new and more prosperous future in the United States.

Likewise, José's parents used to work for a polymer company in Mexico City before they moved here. However, after their business failed and they had no income, they decided to sell everything, including their house, to immigrate to the United States.

R.V.: Tell me about your parents' education.

José: My dad *solamente estudio hasta la secundaria* … which is middle school, *pero quería estudiar más*. And then *la mamá de mi papá le dijo que no que se pusiera a trabajar. Porque la mamá de mi papá tuvo 8 hijos* and then *los hermanos menores de mi papá eran como unos tres y como mis abuelitos se separaron, mi abuelito se la pasaba tomando y mi abuelita iba mucho a la iglesia, entonces a mi papá le tocaba trabajar, como sus hermanos mayores ya se habían casado y vivían en Norte Carolina, mi papá le tocó trabajar y se metió al ejército. So na' más estudió hasta la secundaria y mi mamá … mis abuelitos, los papas de mi mamá, si tenían dinero, pero mi mamá no quiso estudiar, sólo estudió hasta el noveno grado yo creo.* (My dad only studied until middle school, but he wanted to study more. And then my dad's mother asked him to work instead. Since my dad's mom had eight children and my dad's younger brothers were like three and my grandparents split, my grandfather used to drink and my grandma used to go to church a lot, then my dad had to work and since my dad's older brothers were already married and were living in North Carolina, my dad had to work and he enlisted in the army. That is why he only studied until middle school and my mom … my grandparents, my mom's parents, they had money, but my mom did not want to study. She only completed ninth grade I guess).

Overall, most of these boys' parents did not have a high school diploma. Carlos's mother was the only one who completed a high school education in this country and Raúl's mother attended nursing school in Puerto Rico but did not complete her studies. Before moving to the United States, most of these boys' parents were poor or working-class citizens. Working to support their parents and younger siblings became more important than getting an education to most of these boys' parents. As a result they lacked education in their native country due to poverty, which limited their access to other social opportunities. For that reason, these boys' parents decided to move to this country. Suárez-Orozco and Suárez-Orozco (2001) state that immigration is a highly stressful process for the family but is worth the sacrifices even when "the gains of immigration come at a considerable cost" (p. 6). Most of these boys' parents left behind other relatives that they will never see again due to their immigration status or countries' political affairs with the United States.

Instead, some immigrant families work long hours to repay their border crossing fees; some others keep saving most of their salaries waiting for the opportunity to bring the rest of the family members to join them even if it means risking their own lives.

However, it does not take that long for immigrants of color to realize that their skin tone, nationality, language, and socioeconomic conditions push them to be on the bottom of the societal structure. Noguera (2008) argues:

> More often than not, Latinos are trapped in the lowest-paying jobs. We are the laborers, the busboys, maids, nannies, gardeners, mechanics, and waiters. We specialize in doing the dirty work—the work U.S.-born Americans reject. We remove asbestos from buildings, we handle toxic waste, and we take care of the sick and the aged. (p. 52)

In order to unpack how these boys' parents' *Otherness* push them to join a *caste minority* status in this country or *círculo de pobreza* (circle of poverty), I asked them what kinds of jobs their parents had once they moved to this country. Pedro's father arrived to this country when he was still very young, but due to his family's socioeconomic situation and a lack of support from schools, he abandoned his school.

Pedro:	My dad, he dropped [school] when he was like a junior and he became a truck driver since then. He's been a truck driver the whole time. My father goes to different states. He spends a lot of time on the road.
Luis:	My dad, he makes furniture. And my mom, I don't know how you call that word, *de medias* [socks] in a factory.
Julio:	My dad, you *Takkis* [chips]? Mexican *Takkis* tortilla chips. He works for that company. The company is in Charlotte but he works around here and all that. He distributes *Takkis*. My mom does nails and put on make-up and stuff in a beauty salon.

I want to highlight that these boys' fathers' jobs kept them away from home for long hours and sometimes days at a time. In previous interviews, Pedro shared that while his parents were still together he never saw his father. Luis's and Julio's parents' jobs were based on production and were seasonal employment, which means they had to work long hours in order to make decent wages. Since their jobs were seasonal, they could be laid off or sent home without any type of benefits. Juan and José's parents were working in factories. Emilio's parents worked at a *tienda* (grocery store); Carlos's mother was unemployed and his father worked in a pizzeria in New Jersey. Raúl's mom was not working since she stayed home taking care of Raúl's stepfather. Like their mothers, these boys' fathers had no choice but to use their time working long hours to support their families financially. Parents' job opportunities in this country have been limited.

These boys' parents' stories of hard work before and after they immigrated to this country represent the communal voice that most Latino/Latina immigrants experience while trying to achieve a better life and future for themselves and their loved ones. The main goal of making more money to support their families here and back home leads most Latino/Latina immigrants to do the dirty jobs that most U.S. citizens are not willing to do. The fact that most of them live in segregated neighborhoods and cannot communicate in the English language becomes the new norm, and many of them continue living in poverty even when they assume that they are making more money than when they were back in their country. Many of them feel fortunate to have a job or jobs that can help them support their family and send their children to school, ignoring that those types of jobs and long working hours will keep them and their family trapped in a *caste minority* status or what I refer to as *círculo de pobreza* (circle of poverty).

Parents' Limited English-Language Skills

My father says when he came to this country he ate *hamandeggs* for three months. Breakfast, lunch and dinner. *Hamandeggs*. That was the only word he knew. He doesn't eat *hamandeggs* anymore. (From *The House on Mango Street* by Sandra Cisneros, 1984, p. 77)

Being undocumented, lacking a formal education and socio-economic status in their home country, and working long hours in this country make it almost impossible for Latino/Latina immigrants to acquire English-language fluency. When immigrants of color are not able to communicate in the privileged language, they become victims of racial stereotypes and marginalization within the dominant culture. Suárez-Orozco and Suárez-Orozco (2001) posit, "Today's immigrants of color are seen by many as possessing traits that make them 'unmeltable' and incompatible with modern American culture like other minority groups such as African Americans and Puerto Ricans" (p. 8). This constant reminder about their racial/ethnic, social, and immigration status pushes immigrants of color to internalize and to accept racism and the other forms of subordination as norms, which leads many to experience isolation and to develop their own behaviors to resist and navigate the dominant culture. I posit that this isolation sometimes deters Latino/Latina immigrants' acquisition of the English language.

When I asked these boys about their parents' education in this country, most of them shared that their parents tried to learn English but due to lack of time and family responsibilities they were not able to learn it.

Raúl: *Mi mamá si ha ido a clases. Tuvo que dejar de ir por algo, pero no me recuerdo porque. No sé si es porque no podía manejar por unas cosas que tiene en las manos que no podía manejar … y también tiene que estar pendiente a mi padrastro que él tiene condiciones del hígado … y como quien dice siempre tiene que estar 24/7 con él.* (My mom used to attend classes. She had to stop going because of something, but I don't remember. I don't know because she could not drive because she had something on her hands that did not let her drive … and also because she has to take care of my stepdad who has some liver problems … and she has to take care of him 24/7).

Luis: My mom has tried … but she never got stick to it. She bought a course but she never used it. I mean at first she tried to use it, but then she never used it again. She got lazy. My dad *kinda* of understand a couple of words and can speak but not fluently.

Julio: My parents couldn't in New York because they were working all the time, so they really didn't have time. When they came here they can, they tried but then they stopped … something like that. I am not sure what happened. They can understand more than they can talk.

Juan: My mother has, my dad doesn't care about it. My mom, she can understand some words, but not all of it. My dad is always working and as soon as he comes home, he wants to eat and then maybe sleep or working night shift or whatever. And he has friends he hangs out with and my mom is always cooking and baby-sitting so she says is hard for them to learn all that's going on.

José: My dad kinda. My mom kinda understand but not really. My dad, yeah. They went to RCC [a local community college], but my dad got another job and my mom, she couldn't 'cause my mom had to pick me up after practice and she works like … I mean she doesn't have time. *Sale a las cinco y media y de ahí y me pasa a recoger* after soccer practice and then *compra algo de comer* and then *en lo que hace la comida ya es como las nueve.* (She gets out of work at five thirty and then she picks me up after soccer practice and then buys something to eat and then by the time she is finished cooking, it is around nine). I mean she doesn't have time.

Emilio: My parents didn't go to any classes. They probably learned it from me, me speaking to my brother in English so they would understand. They would ask me what such and such mean and I would explain it to them and just over time it's just English. They are not fluent, just sort of. They just understand words, can you do this? Okay, stuff like that. They know basic English.

What mainstream society ignores is that most of these poor and working-class immigrants' first priority is to find a decent job to support their children. The fact is that most of them earn low wages and work long hours or have two or three jobs; this does not give them time to receive formal instruction to acquire the new language. Some parents prefer to work long hours or more than one job and let their children learn the English language at school, giving the children a new role as cultural broker in the school and the community. It is important to note also that working long hours, taking care of children, and taking English lessons can represent impossible obstacles for Latina mothers to overcome. Most of the participants shared that their mothers are the only adult in the family, so their mothers' responsibility to support and to take care of them becomes their number one priority. Although some Latino/Latina parents find time to learn English, the fact that some of them possess little or no education in their heritage language, or had unprepared English as a Second Language teachers, makes it even more difficult for them to learn the privileged language.

Due to their lack of literacy skills in their native language and illiteracy in the English language, most of them have no choice but to accept discrimination and isolation from the main society as norms. Most of the time it has been their children who advocate for them and other relatives since they learned to communicate in English and use their Spanish heritage language as part of their linguistic capital to support their *familias*.

Conclusion

Being illiterate in their heritage language represents a gigantic hurdle that immigrants of color have to face once they arrive in this country. Then after entering the United States, most of them have to learn how to cope with racism, classism, and other layers of subordination. Most of these new immigrants of color end up trapped in a *caste minority* status, making low salaries, alienated in their own communities, and/or living in the shadows for fear of deportation or feeling unwelcome for representing the *Other*. Although most immigrants of color develop their own sense of community in their grocery stores, churches, and work places, they are still oppressed and marginalized by the dominant culture.

Even before they complete their high school education, those who make it, most Latino boys already know what kinds of jobs they will be doing regardless of their immigration status. Many Latino boys and men end up working in construction sites, factories, fast food restaurants, or landscaping. Most of those boys who finish high school do not see higher education as an ultimate option. Instead, they decide to start having their own families or to support younger siblings, parents, or other relatives back home. Others get trapped in gangs or illicit activities. By breaking the law, some of them end up in prison or dead before they reach adulthood.

I posit that as long as this colorblind system sees Latino boys' lack of academic achievement and Latino men's low-wage jobs as norms, many Latino boys and men will not see their education as a hope that can enable them to obtain upward mobility in society. "Hope is the single trait that cuts across at least the initial stages of all immigrants" (Suárez-Orozco & Suárez-Orozco, 2001, p. 122), and when that hope is gone, immigrants plant that hope in their new generation. Then their new hope relies on their children's access to a better education and upward mobility in society. Unfortunately, that new hope becomes a utopia when the new generation becomes aware of their *caste minority* status and internalizes it as the norm. Breaking that *caste minority* status puts some Latino/Latina teenagers in a very difficult position, sometimes pitting them against their own group. A few of them decide to challenge society's expectations leaving their loved ones behind in order to succeed academically or to experience social upward mobility, while most of them prefer to stay around their parents, friends, and other relatives and accept their social status as their only path.

· 6 ·

CONCLUSIONS

CHAPEL HILL—After riding a cattle train through Mexico, Emilio Vicente, his mother and several others climbed under barbed wire at the Arizona border in 1997.

They had come from Guatemala, and Emilio, then 6, had no concept of the danger when the group entered the United States illegally. The journey, he said, was an adventure with a purpose.

The boy was making a trip, in his mind, to meet his dad. He had not seen his father since he was a baby, and had no memory of the man. His father had gone to America seeking a better life, and he had found a place for his family in Siler City, where a giant poultry processor offered jobs, and maybe a future.

Now, Emilio Vicente is on another journey with a purpose. On Tuesday, he will be on a the ballot for student body president at UNC-Chapel Hill, where his candidacy has drawn national interest at a time when an immigration overhaul may be gaining momentum in Washington. (Stancill, 2014, paras. 1–4)

Introduction

Emilio Vicente's story of hard work and resiliency echoes the participants' narratives in this ethnographic study. Through family support, sacrifice, and hard work, Emilio found the network support through a mentoring program at UNC-Chapel Hill that prepared him to challenge social/school norms and immigration policies. Like Emilio, in my study, nine Latino teenage boys voiced the communal experiences of many other Latino teenage boys navigating and resisting the U.S. school system. I unearth how public education policies and school reforms keep teachers and school administrators trapped in a structural system, perpetuating colorblindness, meritocracy, and inequity. I unpack how through a deficit-thinking model in education Communities of Color are still analyzed as culturally deficient. This book also unpacks how these students' experiences with social identities such as gender, race, ethnicity, class, immigration status, and phenotype intersected racism as well as other layers of oppression, shaping their lives as boys and men of color. Finally, while unveiling these boys' parents' stories of immigration, socio-economic status, and English-language acquisition, I discuss how these social issues shaped these boys' educational experiences and well-being.

Findings from this book reveal how these Latino teenage boys used their community cultural wealth (CCW) as the main core to build resiliency and to develop a network orientation while remaining in school. The purpose of this chapter is to discuss the significance of the findings from the previous chapters. First, I will answer each research question. Then I will answer my research purpose. Next, I will explain how my book filled the gap in the literature, followed by the limitations and possibilities. Finally, I will conclude with some final thoughts about some suggestions for teaching Latino boys and future studies on Latino boys and men in this country.

Book Questions

Using critical race theory (CRT), Latino critical theory (LatCrit), and Chicano/Chicana epistemologies, I answered the research questions that guided my book. First, I wanted to know, *How do educational structures, practices, and discourses perpetuate elements of colorblindness, meritocracy, race neutrality, and inequality among Latino teenage boys?* Even though my book focused on Latino teenage boys, through my observations and teachers' interviews, I analyzed how an institutionalized, colorblind, school system pushed most students, especially students of color, to conform to their teachers' low expectations, and a white-dominant culture. Giroux (2010) claims

colorblindness does not deny the existence of race; it nullifies the claim that race is responsible for alleged injustices that reproduce group inequalities, privilege whites, and negatively affect economic mobility, the possession of social resources, and the acquisition of political power. (p. 87)

It is an institutionalized colorblind school structure that denies most students of color access to the real purpose of a democratic education and and the ability to experience social upward mobility.

In Chapter 2, I discussed teachers' low expectations of Latino students. I asked Pedro about how much he liked his English class. He stated, "Ms. Dixon doesn't really teach English; she only teaches us assignment and just go and do it. And that's it, that's not really—she doesn't really pay attention to us. That's what I think." Like Pedro, Luis also added, "Yes, like when teaching is just talking and talking about the subject ... like to me, I like to do hands-on activities. And I feel like if she teaches me for a little bit and I work on it a little bit and then she teaches and I work some more on it, then I get stuff better like that." These boys were consciously aware of the kind of teaching they were receiving. They learned that in order to succeed in school, they had to follow their teachers' unchallenging assignments and lectures. Even though Pedro's comments represented valuable insights for the purpose of this study, it is important to realize how public school teachers and administrators are caught in school reforms and policies that promote inequity in education. Giroux (2012b) claims,

> Teachers are no longer asked to think critically and be creative in the classroom. On the contrary, they are now forced to simply implement predetermined instructional procedures and standardized content at best and at worst put their imaginative powers on hold while using precious classroom time to teach students how to master the skill of test taking. (p. 2)

These new school policies and reforms lead most public school teachers to promote inequity by not encouraging teachers to meet individual students' needs. Teachers' classroom performance is primarily focused on teaching-to-the-test methods, standardized benchmarks, end-of-course tests, and strict discipline practices. For instance, the fact that this school system had recently purchased laptops for every student through grant money discouraged teachers from preparing their own lessons; instead they often relied upon software programs with already-made lessons and assessments. This technology-based initiative also led many teachers to recycle their lessons, perpetuating inequity through a banking method (lecturing and copying from slides) and a one-size-fits-all (online) assessment. Giroux (2012b) claims, "teachers are forced to adopt an educational vision and philosophy that has little respect for the empowering possibilities of either knowledge or critical classroom practices" (p. 3). In this school, all students were expected to complete and to submit their assignments online and usually from home, ignoring issues of socioeconomic status. Giroux (2012b) adds, "in some public schools students are turning up for classes in which teachers are completely absent, replaced by computers, offering online modes of education" (p. 4). The computers added an extra layer of distance between the students and teachers. In addition, the computer-based requirements became a source of inequity; most working-class and poor minorities, especially Latino/Latina families, did not have access to the Internet at home and many could not stay after school to work on their online assignments due to lack of transportation or family responsibilities.

During my teaching experience and classroom observations, I noticed how low-performing students, usually boys of color, got distracted while using their laptops. It was always a struggle to make sure they focused on their assignments. Even though the classrooms were quiet and discipline was not an issue, a lot of students used their computers for personal entertainment. When a student was caught using his/her computer inappropriately, he/she had to return it back to the media center. The student's name was put on a restricted list and had to pick up his computer before class and return it after school. This system made it even more difficult for most students to complete their assignments at home. However, the biggest example of inequality occurred when students broke their computers. I witnessed many poor minority parents getting upset and/or returning the computers back to school because they could not afford to pay for the computer damage. Some parents claimed that they never asked for their children to have a computer at home; others returned after they realized their children were not using it at home for school assignments. Even though the use of technology was a school-wide teaching initiative, those who got in trouble for "breaking the rules" while using the laptops were mostly boys of color. What teachers and school administrators did not recognize was the fact that most of these boys had never had access to a computer before or never used it as a school-learning tool. As a result, some of them relished the opportunity to play video games, watch videos, and socialize on social media; they chose this previously unavailable resource to enjoy what many other teens do. The temptation overrode their desire to follow instructions that prepared them to master standardized tests or to complete pre-fabricated and/or culturally biased lessons.

The fact that boys of color were always punished for not following school rules was understood as boys breaking school rules; however, it served to perpetuate inequity and colorblindness in the educational system. To high-light in-depth the experiences of these students as boys of color in education, my second research questions asked: *How do the interrelation of racism, gender discrimination, and other forms of subordination shape the educational experiences of Latino teenage boys?* During the first conversation, I asked these boys if they believed their ethnicity influenced how they did in school. Most of them shared that being Latino or Hispanic had nothing to do with how they did in school. Luis shared, "It depends on the person because there are other kids that … they're the same as me but they do better. I guess they push themselves some more … it might just depend on the individual himself." Most of them felt it was a personal choice; however, this was an initial reaction. When questioned more deeply they had more complex answers.

As I continued with my book, during our second conversations, I asked more specific questions that led the students to critically voice issues of racism, gender discrimination, and other forms of subordination in school. In Chapter 2, I unearthed some of the most common barriers these boys faced that shaped their school and personal lives. Even though most students viewed gang activities as something of the past or that they never heard about, Alex admitted to joining a gang due to the fact that his brothers were also gang members. Other students shared that their parents and other relatives talked to them about the dangers of being a gang member. For example, Juan shared that being a gang member was "stupid" since boys did it to gain acceptance from their peers. Although all but one of these boys had never been in a gang, and most stated that they never heard about gangs in high school, they were aware that being Latino boys made them vulnerable to be viewed as gang members by teachers, school administrators, and the law.

Contrary to what these boys shared in their counternarratives, when I talked with teachers about some of the most common problems in school among Latino boys, most of them recognized that gang related problems had decreased compared to previous years and that more Latino/Latina students were graduating from high school. However, they also recognized that Latino teenage boys dealt with more problems at school when compared to Latina girls. When I asked teachers what was the biggest challenge while teaching Latino teenage boys, most of them agreed that gangs were still a problem; others shared that motivational factors, teen pregnancy, work, attendance, and resistance to following school rules prevented Latino boys from obtaining a high school diploma. Some of them shared having some Latino students who got in trouble with the law and dropped out of school. Mr. Otto said, "I know of one student in particular that dropped out because he was involved in gang violence ... gang activity ... and break-in and entering, he got in trouble with the law; actually he got out of jail yesterday." None of these teachers acknowledged how the school culture and curriculum, as well as their low expectations through their lecturing and unchallenging assignments made students experience lack of motivation and engagement. Instead, these teachers blamed it on students' parents' lack of responsibility and their culture as the reasons why Latino students did not succeed academically. Mr. Sanchez shared:

> Many times they come from rough home lives or they don't have very good role models or one of their parents is ... either they left or work, or they didn't live with their parents, either one of them, but especially if the male figure is missing in their lives, because they lack that guidance that most of the time the father is usually the one would be in charge of giving the best advice to their teenage boy ... so I guess I could say that the biggest challenge would be to help them see the value of education and how important that is in their lives if they take advantage of it, how education can help them access a better future.

Mr. Sanchez's interpretation of Latino students' failure is related to a lack of parental support or a male role model at home. Using his male privilege position, he argued that the lack of a father figure contributes to a boy's academic failure. In addition, he blamed the students for not taking advantage of the U.S. school system to improve their lives; this aligns with the myth of meritocracy, that only hard work is needed. According to Mr. Sanchez, it is the Latino boys' parents and their lack of motivation that prevents their academic success.

Like Mr. Sanchez, when I asked Ms. Dixon if she knew the reasons why Latino boys dropped out of school more than Latina girls, she associated it with the students' family responsibilities. She posited:

> There's this really strong need to take care of other people and they feel a strong responsibility within the family and so ... I noticed even like caring for younger brothers and sisters and things like that and ... I mean those who work are sure that their brothers and sisters have the best clothes and the nicer things, I guess I think like a family responsibility to where they see the family struggle or they see someone in the family not having as much as other people and they try to equalize that.

Even though Ms. Dixon acknowledged that she did not fully understand the students' culture, she assumed that the reason why Latino students dropped out of school was associated more to their culture than to the school. Moreover, Ms. Dixon failed to address how a colorblind school system and culture also creates barriers that affect the possibilities for Latino boys to remain in school. Giroux (2010) claims,

> If one effect of color-blindness is to deny racial hierarchies, another is to offer whites the beliefs that America is now a level playing field and that the success that whites enjoy relative to minorities of color is largely due to individual determination; a strong ethic, high moral values, and a sound investment in education. (p. 88)

Like Ms. Dixon, Ms. Wolf blamed minority parents' lack of support at school and their roles at home as the reasons why boys have more discipline problems at school. She commented:

> Here is definitely more male than female … is more minority than non … a lot because of the parent involvement … we cannot get in touch with the parent, we cannot make the parent to come in, so we cannot have that parent contact and I think the more extreme they go, the better the chances will come in. I don't know … but definitely it's a male thing and it's definitely minority targeted here. I see a lot of students [white] get out of stuff because their parents get here and involved and I guess it's because discipline is an issue that's supposed to be handled at home, they're going to assume that if the parent comes in and confirms that he will handle it at home, they feel it's covered so they don't cover it scholastically which is actually opening the gap because if a kid has a parent who's concerned about the discipline at home it's a parent who's also concerned about the work ethics at home so they're gonna be doing their work, but if you punished a kid in class for being disruptive, by missing class and that's adding to the gap, that doesn't make any sense.

Again, Ms. Wolf blamed minority parents for not coming to school to advocate for their children. Moreover, she failed to recognize how many of those parents may not possess the social capital to navigate the school culture. Ms. Wolf did not acknowledge that some minority parents are afraid to go to the school because it is the norm that teachers, school administrators, and staff only call parents when their children have done something bad. In the case of new immigrant parents, most of them feel disrespectful asking teachers about their teaching methods and classroom discipline management. For many immigrant parents, a teacher is seen as a professional who deserves the same respect that they do at home. It entitles teachers to do whatever they feel is better for the child; however, it is not always the case.

It is not that minority parents are not concerned about their children's discipline and education; it is the lack of support from teachers, school administrators, and staff, and a colorblind system that ignores the contributions of minorities of color in this country. It is the lack of culturally relevant policies to develop a positive communication bridge between Latino/Latina parents and the school administration that keeps minority parents from feeling welcome in the school building. I provide some suggestions further on in this chapter.

In order to dismantle issues of race neutrality and inequality among Latino teenage boys, I asked these teachers what differences they saw regarding who got punished more in school based on race/ethnicity and gender. Even though they recognized that Black and Latino boys were punished more than white boys, these teachers never acknowledged how these practices were connected to issues of race, gender, and inequality in education. Instead, they accepted it as normal that Black and Latino boys always broke the school rules. Mr. Otto said:

> Boys more than girls obviously but I think that boys ... [thinking] ... in particular boys sometimes try to bend the rules, dress code violation, maybe cellphone type violation ... and then boys are ... are challenged in terms of their reputation, school teachers and administrators have the tendency to buy back and obviously lead to repercussions ... attendance wise it does seem too that minorities in school have problems with attendance, and I don't know the reasons why, but being that I cover ISS [in-school suspension], I like to go through the write-ups and a lot of them are dress code violation and a lot of them are attendance issues, tardies, multiple absences or skipping, those type of things and those seem to be minorities and I don't know the reason why ... I don't know why they are not going to class on time or not showing up to school on time for those reasons. [Prompted] African Americans and Hispanics ... I don't feel our school in particular stereotypes and treats minorities different than the white students, I don't feel like they do, but you know you're asking one teacher ... me personally I hope people think that I don't, but if it happens I think that's a shame ... that they would be treated like that. I would hope that our discipline at our school is consistent regardless of race and gender. Dress code violation ... for one reason or another [he laughs] is seems like ... African American and maybe Hispanic students like to ... break dress code violation ... I don't see a lot of white males with saggy pants, I see a lot of African Americans and some Hispanic boys with saggy pants and that's a particular rule that we try to correct at school ... that's for boys, girls dress code violation is not usually an issue. That seems to be one that we try to clean up for a couple of years, and that seems to be one of them. Like I said I don't typically see white boys with saggy pants in our school ... I don't know if it's just a trend ... a fashion trend or what.

Mr. Otto's comments reveal how through a meritocratic lens minorities are targeted as deficient when compared to a white dominant culture. His comments and experiences in the discipline room show how Black and Latino boys are punished more than white students for breaking school rules, perpetuating the idea of boys and men of color as resistant and rule breakers. Interestingly, he mentioned, "I would hope that our discipline at our school is consistent regardless of race and gender." However, it is clear that boys of color are targeted more than other boys in school. Giroux (2010) claims, "school has become a model for a punishing society in which children who violate a rule as minor as a dress code or slightly act out in class can be handcuffed, booked, and put in a jail cell" (p. 75). In addition, Mr. Otto ignored that when a white dominant culture is imposed on minorities of color, especially boys, they sometimes act out as a form resistance and survival against school authorities even when the outcomes are negative for them.

In Chapter 3, I analyzed how these boys' counternarratives on motivational factors to remain in school were related to a network orientation. I unpacked how these boys' parents and friends instilled in them to *echarle ganas* (do your best) to have a better career and future. Through the use of *consejos* (advice) based on lived experiences, these boys' parents and friends teach them to become resilient. For instance, I discussed how Luis received his parents' support after he became a father even when he got suspended for breaking school rules. Alex, who was targeted many times as a gang member, decided to stay in school because he wanted to make his mother and siblings feel proud. Carlos's reason for staying in school came from his father who always checked on him and his grades at school even though he was not physically living with him. Juan's network orientation came from his friends Rosa and Sarah. Rosa, a Latina woman, helped Juan to navigate the community library where he developed a nurturing and caring support system that motivated him to excel academically. Even though Juan was aware that due to his immigration status in this country he could not pursue higher education, his resiliency and network support helped him to stay focused on his studies. Sports became another important resource to keep these boys in school. Some of them shared how they gained access to other spaces and met new friends due to their athletic skills. Contrary to what these boys' teachers commented in my study, majoritarian assumptions, and cultural deficit models on Communities of Color, these boys' community cultural wealth represented the springboard for them to remain in school. It was their parental and friends' support that encouraged them to focus on their studies. Even though they became critically aware that issues of race, gender, and other forms of discrimination were embedded within the school culture, their cultural capital and network support helped them to become resilient. For example, *familia* was very instrumental for these boys' school motivation. Although previous studies in Mexican and Latino immigrants claim that *familism* does not always equate in immigrant children's academic success (De Genova & Ramos-Zayas, 2003; Stanton-Salazar, 2001; Suárez-Orozco & Suárez-Orozco, 2001; Suárez-Orozco et al., 2008; Valdés, 1996), my study proved different. These boys agreed that the main motivation for remaining in school came from their parents. Most of them felt a moral responsibility for doing their best academically. They narrated how their parents kept instilling in them the importance of *echarle ganas* (doing their best) in school so they could have a better future. Their parents' immigration histories and sacrifices became the driving force for them to strive for academic success and to remain in school. Some of them shared how they represented their family's future and how committed they were to their parents and siblings. Alex, Emilio, José, and Pedro shared how their mothers' suffering encouraged them to work hard. Luis expressed how his father used his life experience as a factory worker to remind him that getting an education was much better than being a low-wage worker.

In the initial conversations, the boys stated that they felt being Latino did not affect their academic performance. Instead, they concluded that it was the individual's choice to do well in school. However, they also stated that as students of color, they were more vulnerable to receive punishment from school authorities than white boys. At the beginning of this study, it was clear that students like Carlos internalized the mainstream idea that Latino students do not care about their education. During my second conversation in Carlos's English honors course, I noticed that out of 24 students only three were boys of color. I observed that these three students were seated at a table by themselves and never interacted with other boys. After this observation, I held the second individual dialogue with Carlos. When I mentioned what I saw in his classroom, he changed his mind about his previous comments about Latinos who do not care about their education. He became consciously aware of how the power of whiteness was embedded within the school culture. He realized that Latino students were always seen as failures and having less potential than white students. Carlos shared,

> I notice like compared to honors classes and regular classes. When I was in regular English, it was a lot of Hispanics there and then when I moved to my honors English, it was less Hispanics, it's like right now there are just three Hispanics there. And I can see the difference.

Even though Carlos noticed that his race determined his success or failure in school, he developed resiliency to think positively about his future. He said,

"And I can see the difference and it inspired me to do better for my culture, my people."

Although the school did not value these boys' cultural capital, these boys' socialization process within their own kinship, peers, and local institutions led them to build a networking support that helped them to remain in school. Stanton-Salazar and Spina (2000) define network orientations as a *help-seeking orientation* in which minority youth make use of a network support to help them cope with life problems.

In Chapter 4, I unpacked how labeling these Latino boys based on their heritage language, skin tone, and gender makes them more vulnerable to punishment and racial profiling in school and their communities. Most of the students agreed that being able to speak Spanish and being brown-skinned boys led them to experience being stereotyped as Mexicans, including assumptions about having an "illegal" status in this country. Carlos and Julio, for example, whose parents came to this country from the Dominican Republic and Colombia, respectively, shared that they were referred to as "Mexicans" for their Spanish speaking skills. Julio shared that for most Americans everyone who speaks Spanish is assumed to be Mexican. Similarly, Carlos added sometimes feeling offended for being referred to as Mexican, especially when one of his teachers made offensive comments about Mexican food, stereotyping Latinos/Latinas as a homogeneous and single culture. Another salient point relates to issues of phenotype and gender threat. José shared how he and his friends were discriminated against at the local mall by the police guards just for being Latinos and speaking Spanish. During the second focus group, most of these boys agreed that boys of color were more vulnerable to being punished at school. When we talked about saggy pants and loose clothes, these boys agreed that teachers and school administrators usually targeted Latino and Black boys more than white boys. They agreed that it was a school norm that boys of color were outcast more than other boys, and there was nothing they could do about it.

After analyzing the multiple barriers these Latino boys encountered while trying to obtain a high school diploma, I also wanted to find out what type of support system encouraged them to remain in school. In my third and final research question, I asked: *How can the community cultural wealth of Latino teenage boys be used as a catalyst to secure their academic success?* Initially, it was my intention to analyze how each capital within these boys' community cultural wealth allowed them to remain in school. As I continued with this book, I discovered that in order to unpack these boys' cultural wealth as an asset for them to remain in school, it was important to simultaneously analyze how resiliency and a network of support was interrelated with these boys' cultural capital.

Book Purpose

This book highlights the counternarratives of nine Latino teenage boys of different social and cultural backgrounds while enrolled in a public high school. The experiences of these boys are examined within the framework of CRT and LatCrit, as well as Chicano/Chicana epistemologies. These counterstories help analyze how racism and other forms of oppression within the educational system shape the educational experiences of historically underrepresented students (in this case, Latino boys). Fernández (2002) states that "By looking to the marginal (and often misunderstood) sociocultural practices of Latino/Latina youth, we get a deeper understanding of how they are oppressed but, at the same time, use their personal agency to resist their social conditions" (p. 48). I analyzed indepth how these students' experiences of race, gender, and other social constructs shaped their identities as boys and men of color.

In my book, I learned that even though these boys represented different cultural Latino backgrounds, most of them shared the same types of discrimination related to issues of race, ethnicity, gender, skin color, social status, English-language acquisition, and immigration status. I learned how these boys internalized race and gender discrimination among boys of color as normal. Most of them agreed school authorities and teachers tend to target them more than white boys because of their race and gender. They argued that racism and discrimination will never go away, and they had to learn to live with it.

Although they claimed that academic success was not related to their ethnicity but to personal choice (meritocracy), they also recognized the fact that most students of color were placed in regular courses as opposed to their white peers who took advanced or college path classes. These students were also aware that their teachers' lectures and low expectations sometimes made them feel unmotivated to achieve academic excellence.

I also learned that teachers' comments focused on Latino students' failure. Most of them never acknowledged their lack of understanding about their students' cultures. Instead, they agreed that Latino boys do not succeed in school due to lack of parental support, a male role model at home, lack of attendance, gang-related problems, teen pregnancy, financial problems, and resistance to school authorities and the law. Most of their comments perpetuated the idea of Communities of Color as culturally deficient, as something that has to be fixed. Most of these teachers agreed that Black and Latino students were punished more than white students; however, they never associated it to racism or gender discrimination, but as students breaking school rules. None of these teachers understood that it was due to a white dominant system that sees communities of color as culturally deficient.

Finally, I learned that these boys' closeness to their family, relatives, and friends were the main reason they kept attending school. I learned that it is within their cultural wealth that these boys developed resiliency. Even though they were conscious about issues of discrimination and inequality, they kept coming to school as a family responsibility and/or moral obligation. Most of them wanted their parents to feel proud of them; others shared that attending school was the best way to pay their parents back for all their sacrifices while coming to this country. Others shared how through their siblings' and friends' mistakes, they wanted to turn their lives into something positive. All of them aspired to either become professionals or to join the military, and all wanted to serve as role models in their families and their communities.

These boys' counterstories allowed me to learn that the main reason why these boys stayed in school was not within the school but outside. It was through their parents, friends, sports, and a local institution in the community that these Latino boys developed their own networks to resist discrimination and other forms of subordination while obtaining a high school diploma.

Filling the Gap in the Literature

Through my book writing, I noted that little information exists that analyzes in depth the personal experiences of Latino teenage boys in education. Even though some scholars and studies mentioned gender differences in education, Latino boys' personal narratives are usually hardly voiced. Most of the studies I encountered about Latinos in education talked about Latina girls, Latinos in higher education, and Latino families. The few studies that I read about Latino boys in education usually talked about negative social issues such as gang affiliation, drugs, parenting, high dropout rates, and discrimination.

This book comes at an important time in today's society and fills a gap in mainstream literature, challenging previous studies on Latinos/Latinas in education that analyzed communities of color as culturally deficient. Similar to Emilio Vicente's story at the beginning of this chapter, my study voices the personal counternarratives of nine Latino teenage boys in high school who learned how to use their cultural capital as a foundation to be resilient and to develop a network of support that allowed them to focus on their education. It is through these boys' counterstorytelling with different layers of discrimination, motivation, resiliency, and support that my study presents this underrepresented group in mainstream cultural studies.

Final Remarks

In June 2012, I decided to quit my job as a high school ESL teacher to focus on my book writing and to gain some experience as a graduate assistant. Since then, I have had mixed feelings about my decision. First, financially it was a big step to adjust to less income and, second, not being able to advocate for my Latino/Latina students on a regular basis made me feel lonely and out of place many times.

Although I am not teaching high school anymore, I still stay in touch with many of my former Latino/Latina students through various social media. This communication line allows me to connect with them and sometimes to give them advice or to share good or bad news with them. They also share with me about their new jobs, newborn babies, break-ups, parties, vacations, and relatives' visits.

After all my years of teaching Latino/Latina students in the Southeast and my studies on Latino boys in high school, I would like to encourage teachers and school administrators to engage in critical dialogues about Latino/Latina students, from pre-K to high school and beyond. Our school systems have to make the curriculum appealing to its diverse population. Teachers and school administrators need to spend more time focusing on students who look and think differently than they do; they also need to engage their students in more critical arguments where minority students can be seen as school assets and not as culturally deficient. In order to allow school administrators to become color conscious, Wise (2010) suggests:

a) End the ability tracking system that limits opportunities of students of color.

b) Advocate for mixed-ability groupings in the classrooms to facilitate cooperative learning.

c) Carry out audits of their school's disciplinary practices to determine the degree of racial disparity in punishments.

d) Train teachers in methods for addressing racial achievement gaps. (pp. 177–178)

Through this process, teachers, school administrators, and other students can overcome stereotypes and generalizations created by the dominant culture. Latino/Latina students need to hear that their cultural capital represents the foundation of their academic and life success. Wise (2010) provides suggestions of actions teachers can take to support students of color:

1. Combine constructive criticism of the work done by students of color with regular consistent reiteration of the teachers' belief in their potential.
2. Encourage group work, team projects, group studying and a collaborative approach to learning, rather than individual work and a competitive approach.
3. Challenge students with high standards, rather than demean them with remediation.
4. All middle schools should strive to enroll Black and Latino students in eighth-grade algebra.
5. Teachers should reject the notion of "aptitude" and stress the malleability of intelligence and ability.
6. Provide "centering" exercises in class that allow students of color to reflect favorably on their identities and values.
7. Get students to see academic success as part of a larger project to undo institutionalized inequity and white supremacy. (pp. 179–182)

Instead of perpetuating the idea that parents of color do not care about their children's education, teachers and administrators need to reach out to Latino/Latina parents in their own communities and find out the reasons why the parents feel excluded from the school system. Valdés (1996) claims that all types of intervention programs to support Latino/Latina families should be focused on understanding, appreciation, and respect of the families. She adds,

> Parents must not be coerced into believing that in order to rear "successful" children, they must give up their childrearing practices that they consider appropriate. They must be helped to understand the alternatives in all of their complexity. They must be made aware of the fact that change in childrearing practices may result in unexpected consequences for their children. (p. 203)

Appreciating and understanding what Latino/Latina parents do at home to support their children's education also allows teachers and parents to develop mutual trust and a communication channel. Even though some Latino/Latina parents seem to be less involved and uninterested in their children's education due to other family responsibilities, work, transportation, illiteracy in their native language or in English, child care, or lack of knowledge with the way school operates, it is the school's responsibility to design and to execute goals that develop a strong community-school partnership.

As an ethnographer, I would also like to encourage future scholars to continue this dialogue with Latino boys and men in education. Noguera and Hurtado (2012) claim that Latino men's lives are hardly portrayed in the media and academia (p. 50). Even though my study showed nine Latino teenage boys who learned how to navigate the U.S. school system, studies should keep exploring the obstacles that prevent most Latino boys and men from finishing high school and beyond. In this book, most teachers agreed that more Latino boys are graduating from high school than before; however, for most of these boys this diploma will not result in a path to higher education or decent jobs after they graduate from high school. This book reveals how these boys learned how to navigate the educational structures of inequity, meritocracy, and colorblindness. All of these boys conformed to a white-dominant school system. This book also unveiled that most of these boys were unprepared to attend higher education or to find better jobs than those who did not graduate. Out of these nine boys, only Emilio and Julio were taking advanced courses that qualified them as college material. Although Juan was an excellent student, his legal status in this country made his future aspirations to attend college more difficult and almost impossible. The rest of the participants had low grades and attended less challenging courses as part of a tracking system where most minority students, especially boys of color, are left unprepared to pursue higher education.

I also discovered that most of these boys were not fully literate in either English or Spanish. Although most of them could communicate in English and Spanish, their literacy levels disqualified them from being fluent in both languages. In addition, based on my study and my interaction with most of my former Latino/Latina students, including those who completed high school and those who dropped out, I did not see a significant difference in outcomes between both groups, especially among Latino boys. In my role as a former teacher in this high school, I learned that most of my former students who graduated from this high school were doing the same types of jobs (landscaping, construction, fast food restaurants, and factories) as those who decided to drop out of school. Some others joined their parents' and relatives' jobs and/or started their own families.

In conclusion, staying in school is not the entire solution, but part of it, since my goal is that more Latino boys graduate from high school and beyond. However, most of those Latino boys who decide to remain in school are not well prepared to pursue higher education or to qualify for better jobs that can allow them to experience upward social mobility. Even when it sounds unobtainable and unrealistic, the U.S. school system needs to develop and to execute school reforms and initiatives that better prepare Latino boys to be positive and active members in a democratic society. I argue that school systems need to stop seeing them as culturally deficient or as "boys will be boys." Instead, school systems need to view Latino boys as promising and capable individuals, representing different stories and life experiences; they need to address these boys' academic needs and life barriers with urgency before society at large accepts their school and life failures as normal.

BIBLIOGRAPHY

Akom, A. A. (2008). Black metropolis and mental life: Beyond the "burden of 'acting white'" toward a third wave of critical racial studies. *Anthropology & Education Quarterly, 39*(3), 247–265.

Alfaro, E. C., Umaña-Taylor, A. J., Gonzales-Backen, M. A., Bámaca, M. Y., & Zeiders, K. H. (2009). Latino adolescents' academic success: The role of discrimination, academic motivation, and gender. *Journal of Adolescence, 32*, 941–962.

Banfield, E. C. (1970). Schooling versus education. In E. C. Banfield, *The unheavenly city: The nature and future of our urban crisis* (pp. 132–157). Boston, MA: Little, Brown.

Bell, D. A. (1992). *Faces at the bottom of the well: The permanence of racism.* New York, NY: Perseus Books Group.

Bernstein, B. (1977). *Class, codes, and control: Vol. 3: Towards a theory of educational transmission.* Boston, MA: Routledge Kegan Paul.

Bettie, J. (2003). *Women without class: Girls, race, and identity.* Berkeley, CA: University of California Press.

Bonilla-Silva, E. (2010). *Racism without racists: Color-blind racism and racial inequality in contemporary America,* (3rd Ed.). Lanham, MD: Rowman & Littlefield Publishers, Inc.

Cammarota, J. (2008). *Sueños Americanos: Barrio youth negotiating social and cultural identities.* Tucson, AZ: University of Arizona Press.

Campos, D. (2013). *Educating Latino boys: An asset-based approach.* Thousand Oaks, CA: Corwin.

Carter, P. L. (2005). *Keepin' it real: School success beyond Black and White.* New York: Oxford University Press.

Chavez, L. R. (2008). *The Latino threat: Constructing immigrants, citizens, and the nation.* Stanford, CA: Stanford University Press.

Cisneros, S. (1984). *The house on Mango Street.* New York, NY: Harper Collins Publisher.

Conchas, G. Q., & Vigil, J. D. (2012). *Streetsmart Schoolsmart: Urban poverty and the education of adolescent boys.* New York, NY: Teachers College Press.

Cuadros, P. (2006). *A home on the field.* New York, NY: Harper Collins.

De Genova, N., & Ramos-Zayas, A. Y. (2003). *Latino crossings: Mexicans, Puerto Ricans, and the politics of race and citizenship.* New York, NY: Routledge.

Delgado Bernal, D. (1998). Using a Chicana feminist epistemology in educational research. *Harvard Educational Review, 68*(4), 555–582.

Delgado Bernal, D. (2002). Critical race theory, Latino critical theory, and critical raced-gendered epistemologies: Recognizing students of color as holders and creators of knowledge. *Qualitative Inquiry, 8*(105), 105–126.

Delgado Bernal, D. (2006). Learning and living pedagogies of the home: The mestiza consciousness of Chicana students. In D. Delgado Bernal, C. A. Elenes, F. E. Godinez, & S. Villenaz (Eds.), *Chicana/Latina education in everyday life: Feminista perspectives on pedagogy and epistemology.* Albany, NY: State University of New York Press.

Delgado, R., & Stefancic, J. (2001). *Critical race theory: The cutting edge.* Philadelphia, PA: Temple University Press.

Delpit, L. D. (2006). *Other people's children: Cultural conflict in the classroom.* New York, NY: New Press.

Delpit, L. D. (2012). *"Multiplication is for white people": Raising expectations for other people's children.* New York, NY: New Press.

Dixson, A. D., & Rousseau, C. K. (2006). And we are not saved: Critical race theory in education ten years later. In A. D. Dixson & C. K. Rousseau (Eds.), *Critical race theory in education: All God's children got a song* (pp. 31–54). New York, NY: Routledge.

Dobson, J. (2001). *Bringing up boys: Practical advice and encouragement for those shaping the next generation of men.* Wheaton, IL: Tyndale House Publishers.

Dunn, L. (1987). *Bilingual Hispanic children on the mainland: A review of research of their cognitive, linguistic, and scholastic development.* Circle Pines, MN: American Guidance Service.

Fernández, L. (2002). Telling stories about school: Using critical race and Latino critical theories to document Latina/Latino education and resistance. *Qualitative Inquiry, 8*(45), 45–65.

Fleischman, P. (2002). *Seedfolks.* New York, NY: Harper Collins.

Flores-González, N. (2002). *School kids/street kids: Identity development in Latino students.* New York, NY: Teachers College Press.

Freire, P. (1998). *Pedagogy of freedom: Ethics, democracy, and civic courage.* Lanham, MD: Rowman & Littlefield.

Gándara, P., & Contreras, F. (2009). *The Latino education crisis: The consequences of failed social politics.* Cambridge, MA: Harvard University Press.

Garcia, E. E. (2001). *Hispanic education in the United States: Raíces y alas.* Lanham, MD: Rowman & Littlefield Publishers, Inc.

Gill, H. (2010). *The Latino migration experience in North Carolina: New roots in the Old North State.* Chapel Hill, NC: The University of North Carolina Press.

Giroux, H. A. (2010). *Politics after hope: Obama and the crisis of youth, race, and democracy.* Boulder, CO: Paradigm.

Giroux, H. A. (2012a). *Disposable youth: Racialized memories and the culture of cruelty.* New York, NY: Routledge.

Giroux, H. A. (2012b). *Education and the crisis of public values: Challenging the assault on teachers, students, & public education.* New York, NY: Routledge.

Glesne, C. (2006). *Becoming qualitative researchers: An introduction.* Boston, MA: Allyn & Bacon.

Heller, C. (1996). *Mexican American youth: Forgotten youth at the crossroads.* New York, NY: Random House.

He, Y., Bettez, S., & Levin, B. B. (2013, April). *Imagined community of education: Voices from refugees and immigrants.* Annual meeting of the American Educational Research Association (AESA), San Francisco, CA.

Hurtado, A., Haney, C. W., & Hurtado, J. G. (2012). "Where the boys are": Macro and micro considerations for the study of young Latino men's educational achievement. In P. Noguera, A. Hurtado, & E. Fergus (Eds.), *Invisible no more: Understanding the disenfranchisement of Latino men and boys* (pp. 101–121). New York, NY: Routledge.

Jensen, A. (1969). How much can we boost I.Q. and scholastic achievement? *Harvard Educational Review, 39,* 1–123.

Jiménez, F. (2001). *Breaking through.* New York, NY: Houghton Mifflin Company.

Ladson-Billings, G. (2009). Just what is critical race theory and what's it doing in a nice field like education? In E. Taylor, D. Gillborn, & G. Ladson-Billings (Eds.), *Foundations of critical race theory* (pp. 17–36). New York, NY: Routledge.

Ladson-Billings, G., & Tate, W. F. IV. (2006). Toward a critical race theory of education. In A. D. Dixson & C. K. Rousseau (Eds.), *Critical race theory in education: All God's children got a song* (pp. 11–30). New York, NY: Routledge.

Lopez, N. (2003). *Hopeful girls, trouble boys: Race and gender disparities in urban education.* New York, NY: Routledge.

Lopez, N. (2012). Racially stigmatized masculinities and empowerment: Conceptualizing and nurturing Latino males' schooling in the United States. In P. Noguera, A. Hurtado, & E. Fergus (Eds.), *Understanding the disenfranchisement of Latino men and boys: Invisible no more* (pp. 235–254). New York, NY: Routledge.

Lugones, M. (2003). *Pilgrimages/Peregrinajes: Theorizing coalition against multiple oppressions.* Lanham, MD: Rowman & Littlefield.

Martinez, V. (1996). *Parrot in the oven: Mi vida.* New York, NY: Harper Collins.

Marx, S. (2006). *Revealing the invisible: Confronting passive racism in teacher education.* New York, NY: Routledge.

Matsuda, M., Lawrence, C., Delgado, R., & Crenshaw, K. (1993). *Words that wound: Critical race theory, assaultive speech, and the First Amendment.* Boulder, CO: Westview.

Menjivar, C. (2005). Central Americans. In S. Oboler & D. J. Gonzalez (Eds.), *The Oxford Encyclopedia of Latinos and Latinas in the United States* (pp. 520–530). Oxford: Oxford University Press.

Moll, L., Amanti, C., Neff, D., & Gonzalez, N. (2009). Funds of knowledge for teaching: Using a qualitative approach to connect homes and classrooms. In N. Gonzalez, L. C. Moll, &

C. Amanti (Eds.), *Funds of knowledge: Theorizing practices in households, communities, and classrooms* (pp. 71–88). New York, NY: Routledge.

Noblit, G. W., Flores, S. Y., & Murillo, E. G. Jr. (2004). *Postcritical ethnography: Reinscribing critique*. Cresskill, NJ: Hampton.

Noguera, P. (2008). *The trouble with Black boys: And other reflections on race, equity, and the future of public education*. San Francisco, CA: Jossey-Bass.

Noguera, P. (2012). Saving black and Latino boys: What schools can do to make a difference. *Phi Delta Kappan, 93*(5), 8–12.

Noguera, P., & Hurtado, A. (2012). Invisible no more: The status and experience of Latino males from multidisciplinary perspectives. In P. Noguera, A. Hurtado, & E. Fergus (Eds.), *Understanding the disenfranchisement of Latino men and boys: Invisible no more* (pp. 1–15). New York, NY: Routledge.

Noguera, P., Hurtado, A., & Fergus, E. (2012). *Understanding the disenfranchisement of Latino men and boys: Invisible no more*. New York, NY: Routledge.

Noguera, P., & Yonemura Wing, J. (2006). *Unfinished business: Closing the racial achievement gap in our schools*. San Francisco, CA: Jossey-Bass.

Ogbu, J. U. (2004). Collective identity and the burden of "Acting White" in Black history, community, and education. *The Urban Review, 36*(1), 1–35.

Pereira, K. M., Fuligni, A., & Potochnick, S. (2010). Fitting in: The roles of social acceptance and discrimination in shaping the academic motivations of Latino youth in the U.S. Southeast. *Journal of Social Issues, 66*(1), 131–153.

Pérez Hubert, L. (2009). Challenging racist nativist framing: Acknowledging the community cultural wealth of undocumented Chicana college students to reframe the immigration debate. *Harvard Educational Review, 79*(4), 704–784.

Pew Hispanic Center. (2011). Retrieved July 13, 2012, from http://www.pewhispanic.org/

Pillow, W. S. (2010). Dangerous reflexivity: Rigour, responsibility and reflexivity in qualitative research. In P. Thomson & M. Walker (Eds.), *The Routledge doctoral students' companion*. New York, NY: Routledge.

Portes, A., & Rumbaut, R. G. (2001). *Legacies: The story of the immigrant second generation*. Los Angeles, CA: University of California Press.

Quintana, S. M., Segura Herrera, T. A., & Nelson, M. L. (2010). Mexican American high school students' ethnic self-concepts and identity. *Journal of Social Issues, 66*(1), 11–28.

Rios, V. M. (2011). *Punished: Policing the lives of Black and Latino boys*. New York, NY: New York University Press.

Rodriguez, R. (2003). *Brown: The last discovery of America*. New York, NY: Penguin Books.

Román, D., & Sandoval, A. (1997). Caught in the web: *Latinidad*, AIDS, and allegory in *Kiss of the Spider Woman*, the Musical. In C. F. Delgado, & J. E. Muñoz, *Everynight life: Culture and dance in Latin/o America* (pp. 254–287). Durham, NC: Duke University Press.

Schwartz, A. (1971). A comparative study of values and achievement: Mexican-American and Anglo-American youth. *Sociology of Education, 44*, 438–462.

Solórzano, D. G., & Delgado Bernal, D. (2001). Examining transformational resistance through a critical race and LatCrit framework: Chicana and Chicano students in an urban context. *Urban Education, 36*(3), 308–342.

Solórzano, D. G., & Villalpaldo, O. (1998). Critical race theory, marginality, and the experience of students of color in higher education. In C. A. Torres & T. R. Mitchell (Eds.), *Sociology of education: Emerging perspectives* (pp. 211–224). Albany, NY: State University of New York Press.

Solórzano, D. G., & Yosso, T. J. (2009). Critical race methodology: Counter-storytelling as an analytical framework for educational research. In E. Taylor, D. Gillborn, & G. Ladson-Billings (Eds.), *Foundations of critical race theory in education* (pp. 131–147). New York, NY: Routledge.

Soto, G. (1994). *Jesse*. New York, NY: Harcourt.

Soto, G. (2006). *Buried onions*. New York, NY: Harcourt.

Stancill, J. (2014, February 8). UNC student's candidacy draws attention as immigration overhauls gains momentum. *News & Observer*. Retrieved February 9, 2014, from http://www.newsobserver.com/2014/02/08/3603256/for-uncs-emilio-vicente-an-extraordinary.html

Stanton-Salazar, R. (1997). A social capital framework for understanding the socialization of racial minority children. *Harvard Educational Review, 67*(1), 1–40.

Stanton-Salazar, R. (2001). *Manufacturing hope and despair: The school and kin support networks of U.S.-Mexican youth*. New York, NY: Teachers College Press.

Stanton-Salazar, R., & Spina, S. U. (2000). The network orientations of highly resilient urban minority youth: A network-analytic account of minority socialization and its educational implications. *The Urban Review, 32*(3), 227–261.

Suárez-Orozco, C., & Suárez-Orozco, M. M. (2001). *Children of immigration*. Cambridge, MA: Harvard University Press.

Suárez-Orozco, C., Suárez-Orozco, M. M., & Todorova, I. (2008). *Learning a new land: Immigrant students in American society*. Cambridge, MA: Belknap Press of Harvard University Press.

Suzuki, L. A., & Valencia, R. R. (1997). Race-ethnicity and measured intelligence: Educational implications. *American Psychologist, 52*(10), 1103–1112.

Tatum, B. D. (1997). *"Why are all the Black kids sitting together in the cafeteria?" and other conversations about race*. New York, NY: BasicBooks.

Tatum, B. D. (2007). *Can we talk about race? And other conversations in an era of school resegregation*. Boston, MA: Beacon Press.

Taylor, E. (2009). The foundations of critical race theory in education: An introduction. In E. Taylor, D. Gillborn, & G. Ladson-Billings (Eds.), *Foundations of critical race theory in education* (pp. 1–13). New York, NY: Routledge.

Taylor, E., Gillborn, D., & Ladson-Billings. G. (Eds.). (2009). *Foundations of critical race theory in education*. New York, NY: Routledge.

Terman, L. (1916). *The measurement of intelligence*. Boston, MA: Houghton Mifflin.

Umaña-Taylor, A. J. (2004). Ethnic identity and self-esteem: Examining the role of social context. *Journal of Adolescence, 27*, 139–146.

Umaña-Taylor, A. J., Gonzales-Backen, M. A., & Guimond, A. B. (2009). Latino adolescents' ethnic identity: Is there a developmental progression and does growth in ethnic identity predict growth in self-esteem? *Child Development, 80*(2), 391–405.

Umaña-Taylor, A. J., & Updergraff, K. A. (2007). Latino adolescents' mental health: Exploring the interrelations among discrimination, ethnic identity, cultural orientation, self-esteem, and depressive symptoms. *Journal of Adolescence, 30,* 549–567.

U.S. Census Bureau. (2008). Retrieved July 13, 2012, from www.census.gov

U.S. Census Bureau, *Statistical Abstract of the United States: 2012.* (2012). Retrieved July 13, 2012, from http://www.census.gov/compendia/statab/2012/tables/12s0271.pdf

Valdés, G. (1996). *Con respeto: Bridging the distance between culturally diverse families and schools: An ethnographic portrait.* New York, NY: Teachers College Press.

Valencia, R. R. (2010). *Dismantling contemporary deficit thinking: Educational thought and practice.* New York, NY: Routledge.

Valencia, R. R., & Black, M. S. (2002). "Mexican Americans don't value education!" On the basis of the myth, mythmaking, and debunking. *Journal of Latinos and Education, 1*(2), 81–103.

Valencia, R. R., & Ronda, M. A. (1994). "At risk" Chicano students: The institutional and communicative life of a category. *Hispanic Journal of Behavioral Sciences, 16*(4), 363–395.

Valencia, R. R., & Solórzano, D. (1997). Contemporary deficit thinking. In R. Valencia (Ed.), *The evolution of deficit thinking in educational thought and practice* (pp. 160–210). New York, NY: Falmer.

Valencia, E. Y., & Johnson, V. (2006). Latino students in North Carolina: Acculturation, perceptions of school environment, and academic aspirations. *Hispanic Journal of Behavioral Sciences, 28*(3), 350–367.

Valenzuela, A. (1999). *Subtractive schooling: U.S.-Mexican youth and the politics of caring.* Albany, NY: State University of New York Press.

Vasquez, L. (2000). *Programs for Hispanic fathers: Perspectives from research.* Retrieved from http://fatherhood.hhs.gov/hispanic01/research.htm

Villenas, S., & Deyhle, D. (1999). Critical race theory and ethnographies challenging the stereotypes: Latino families, schooling, resilience and resistance. *Curriculum Inquiry, 29*(4), 413–445.

West, C. (2001). *Race matters.* Boston, MA: Beacon Press.

West, C. (2004). *Democracy matters: Winning the fight against imperialism.* New York, NY: Penguin Books.

West, C. (2011). *Hope on a tightrope* (3rd ed.). Carlsbad, CA: Hay House.

Wise, T. (2010). *Colorblind: The rise of post-racial politics and the retreat from racial equity.* San Francisco, CA: City Lights Books.

Yosso, T. J. (2006a). *Critical race counterstories along the Chicana/Chicano educational pipeline.* New York, NY: Routledge.

Yosso, T. J. (2006b). Whose culture has capital? A critical race theory discussion of community cultural wealth. In A. D. Dixson & C. K. Rousseau (Eds.), *Critical race theory in education: All God's children got a song* (pp. 167–189). New York, NY: Routledge.

Yosso, T. J., Smith, W. A., Ceja, M., & Solórzano, D. G. (2009). Critical race theory, racial microaggressions, and campus racial climate for Latina/o undergraduates. *Harvard Educational Review, 79*(4), 659–690.

Yosso, T. J., Villalpando, O., Delgado Bernal, D., & Solórzano, D. G. (2001). Critical race theory in Chicano/a education. *National Association for Chicano and Chicana Studies Annual Conference*. Paper 9.

Zamudio, M., Russell, C., Rios, F. A., & Bridgeman, J. L. (2011). *Critical race theory matters: Education and ideology*. New York, NY: Routledge.

Zarate, M. E., Bhimji, F., & Reese, L. (2005). Ethnic identity and academic achievement among Latino/a adolescents. *Journal of Latinos and Education, 4*(2), 95–114.

Critical Studies of LATINOS/AS in the Americas

Yolanda Medina and Margarita Machado-Casas
GENERAL EDITORS

Critical Studies of Latinos/as in the Americas is a provocative interdisciplinary series that offers a critical space for reflection and questioning what it means to be Latino/a living in the Americas in twenty-first century social, cultural, economic, and political arenas. The series looks forward to extending the dialogue to include the North and South Western hemispheric relations that are prevalent in the field of global studies.

Topics that explore and advance research and scholarship on contemporary topics and issues related with processes of racialization, economic exploitation, health, education, transnationalism, immigration, gendered and sexual identities, and disabilities that are not commonly highlighted in the current Latino/a Studies literature as well as the multitude of socio, cultural, economic, and political progress among the Latinos/as in the Americas are welcome.

To receive more information about CSLA, please contact:

Yolanda Medina (ymedina@bmcc.cuny.edu) &
Margarita Machado-Casas (Margarita.MachadoCasas@utsa.edu)

To order other books in this series, please contact our Customer Service Department at:

(800) 770-LANG (within the U.S.)
(212) 647-7706 (outside the U.S.)
(212) 647-7707 FAX

Or browse online by series at:

WWW.PETERLANG.COM